SOLENT
Creeks, Craft & Cargoes

Michael Langley

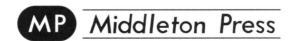

MP Middleton Press

Cover pictures: *Upper left - caption no. 119*
Lower - caption no. 166
Upper right - caption no. 26
Middle right - caption no. 141

Notes about the author -

Great Grandfather Langley had migrated to the Isle of Wight in the mid 1800s, later and usually in search of better employment prospects, other family members travelled in the opposite direction. The author was born at Horsham, West Sussex and therefore in Island 'parlance' will always be known as an 'overner'. Frequent cross-Solent journeys for holidays and family gatherings doubtless were the catalyst for a life-long interest in maritime affairs. A career followed in ocean shipping within the P&O Group of Companies and a Masters Certificate was obtained in 1975, later leading to shore based employment in Ship Management. This terminated in the early 1990s, when the author himself migrated to the Island and that early interest in local and coastal shipping re-activated, culminating in book one-'SUSSEX SHIPPING- Sail, Steam & Motor'.

Published March 2005

ISBN 1 904474 52 7

© Middleton Press, 2005

Design Deborah Esher

Published by
        Middleton Press
        Easebourne Lane
        Midhurst, West Sussex
        GU29 9AZ
Tel: 01730 813169
Fax: 01730 812601
Email: info@middletonpress.co.uk
www.middletonpress.co.uk

Printed & bound by Biddles Ltd, Kings Lynn

CONTENTS

Preface	3	The craft and locations	6-154
Glossary and Abbreviations	3	Bibliography	155
General Map	4-5	Index	156
Introduction	4	Acknowledgements	159

PREFACE

Not so long ago, goods and travellers cross-Solent had to contend with the irregular wind and tide restrained timings of small commercial sailing craft, such as ketches, cutters and barges.

The steam era saw a sudden mushrooming of ferry services for passengers and mail, and a comparable growth in the freight carrying ability of cargo craft employed. Today, most freight simply utilises the now global roll-on, roll-off system, affording door to door transit without the need for man-handling en-route.

This method, seen from any standpoint is very efficient, but has meant the demise of all but a few minor wharves to commercial traffic.

Chichester and Poole Harbours may not seem immediately relevant to the book, however, they were regular destinations for the smaller local Solent area craft, hence their inclusion.

GLOSSARY & ABBREVIATIONS

----	Sailing ships / un-powered craft		PT	Paddle Tug
DEPV	Diesel Electric Paddle Vessel		SL	Steam Launch
MB	Motor Barge		SS	Steam Ship
MT	Motor Tanker / Motor Tug		SY	Steam Yacht
MV	Motor Vessel		THV	Trinity House Vessel
PS	Paddle Steamer		TSS	Twin Screw Steam Ship

Note: Vessels engaged in fishing are not generally described in this book.

Tonnages:

Net Registered Tonnage, abbr. **nrt**:- earlier sailing ship criteria for measuring hold capacity. Original derivation from wine trade- 'tuns', or barrel capacity. May also appear as **Reg.Tons**.

Gross Registered Tons, abbr. **grt**:- volumetric measure of all enclosed space applied to all ships - i.e. 100cu.ft. = 1 gross ton.

Deadweight Tonnage, abbr. **dwt**:- an indication of the vessels carrying capacity in tons, includes fuel, stores and cargo, etc.

Length overall:	loa	Measurement to the fore and aft extremities.
Beam or breadth:	br.	Measurement to the widest and aft extremities.
Draught:	dr.	Depth of water required for flotation.

Horse Power, engines:

SHP   Shaft Horse Power - usually given for steam ships.

BHP   Brake Horse Power - usually given for motor ships.

Knots: Speed in nautical miles per hour (6080 ft.)

Spring Tides: fortnightly periods of greater tidal range - 'higher' high water 'lower' low water.

Neap Tides;   intervening periods of lesser tidal range - 'lower' high water 'higher' low water.

INTRODUCTION

The development and growth in ocean trades and the ships so employed, have been well described down the years. Giant container ships, car carriers, cruise vessels and tankers are now 'bread and butter' for the Port of Southampton. Similarly, the Royal Navy's fleet and Portsmouth home have seldom been far from the public eye and, more recently, this harbour has seen much expansion in cross-Channel 'super-ferry' operations. It is the aim of this book to examine the myriad of interesting smaller craft, able by their lesser dimensions to serve the district's remoter wharves, creeks and rivers.

Over the last one hundred and fifty years or so, such vessels have made an enormous and very important contribution to industrial growth and public mobility throughout the region. Generally unsung, the exploits and longevity of these often locally constructed craft, and their skilled, hard worked crews were remarkable. By visiting each location in turn, a little of the trade and activity involved is herein described and illustrated, utilising photographs from the 1880s, to the present.

A particular emphasis has been placed on traffic to and from the Isle of Wight, until the early 1800s the preserve of small sailing cargo vessels, mostly locally built, owned and operated. The sudden proliferation of piers and paddle steamers in the first few decades of the 19th century brought great benefits. No longer did the small numbers of travelling public need to be ferried on boatmen's shoulders for the last few yards, across the mud, to dry land.

Steam power and Victorian railway expansion saw an enormous increase in the industrial appetite for coal, soon necessitating proper wharves and handling facilities for such cargoes. In fact, the close relationship between railways and the coal trade would last for well over a century.

The majority of the population had previously been unable to stray far from their immediate localities prior to the Victorian era. Suddenly, affordable railway fares lead to the delights of excursion steamer trips and, for the more serious travellers, greater ease to conduct business, wherever. Mobility had well and truly arrived.

Before 1928, anyone bold enough to transport their motor car cross-Solent had to drive down a slipway, to board a 'tow-boat'. These craft were hinged-stern, dumb barges, towed by steam tugs or paddle steamers. Each barge could carry a few cars or carts, small commercial vehicles (there were no large ones), groups of farm livestock, etc; which undoubtedly made for an interesting passage, since the vagaries of wind and particularly tide ensured erratic, infrequent services and lengthy trips.

In 1928 the first purpose built double ended, ramped motor ferries appeared under Southern Railway's far sighted vision of the future. Dedicated roll-on, roll-off terminals had arrived, but were miniscule in scale compared to the sophisticated facilities required for today's 3,000 ton, half hourly service giants.

A number of the ships illustrated and described herein are specially included as their presence down the years, whilst voyaging through the waters of the Solent, has made an interesting contrast to the well known larger ocean traders. Locally, a mere fifty years ago, 100 ton barge loads of cargo were still economically viable. Today, it is quite unusual to encounter coastal traders carrying less than 1,500 tons of bulk cargo. Just about all other commodities now fall into the global containerisation system, allied to roll-on, roll-off ferry services around Europe and cross-Solent, for final delivery.

Starting at Chichester in the east, the reader is guided westwards along the Mainland shore to Poole, and thence the Isle of Wight. Each location has its map to assist 'navigation'. A special section describes the once prolific ship building and oyster dredging business of Emsworth's J.D.Foster & Co. As we start the 21st century, yachts, their marinas and the leisure industry predominate at the majority of the locations visited, where once thriving commercial centres employed so many.

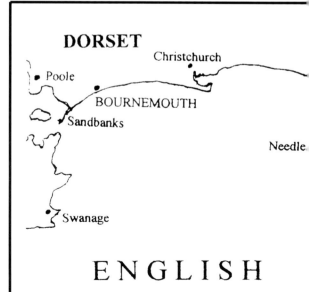

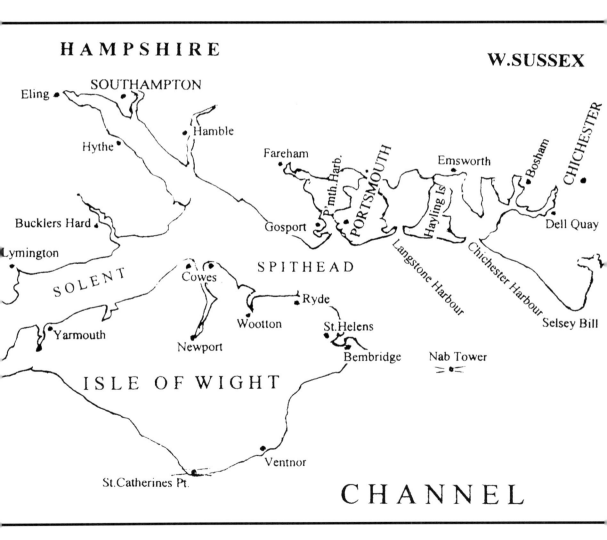

Map No.1 Chichester Harbour

(1) Salterns Lock: access to Southgate Basin, Chichester via the Canal to sea.

(2) Track of the Portsmouth to Arundel Canal, disused by 1850, running eastwards to the River Arun at Ford.

(3) Chichester City Dock, Southgate Basin commercially active 1822-1906.

(4) Dell Quay

(5) Bosham Quay

(6) Emsworth- Fosters Shipyard-oyster trade

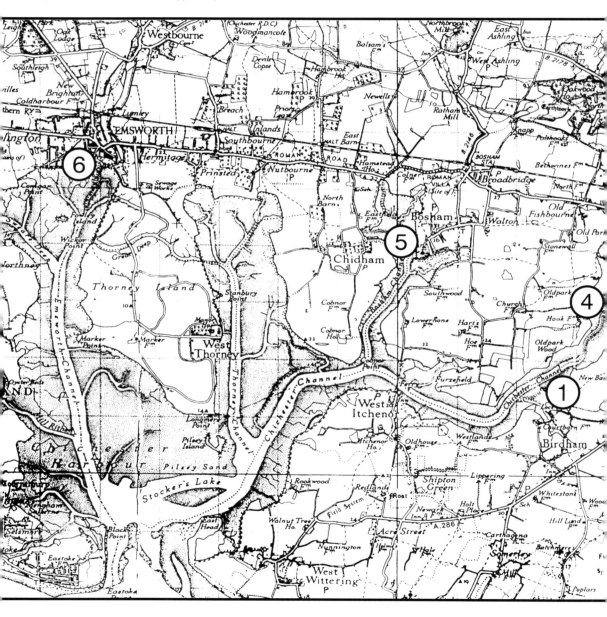

Chichester City Dock-Southgate Basin

A short branch northwards from the Portsmouth to Arundel Canal opened in 1822, to the heart of Chichester at Southgate Basin. From the Salterns Lock there was access to the tidal and shallow expanse of Chichester Harbour and the sea; the engineering works involved were of a minor nature. This ultimately ensured a premature end to traffic, as vessels of approximately 100 tons only could transport freight on the waterway.

By 1906, with increasing competition from Chichester's railway yards, Southgate Basin discovered commercial obsolescence, and closed to shipping. The one true mainstay cargo had been coal for the local gasworks and even this commodity had frequently been subject to transhipment into barges for the final four mile journey. This latter operation would have been labour intensive and costly, closure being inevitable.

Today, the Canal is sadly truncated by modern roadways at Cashers Lock, leaving only a short section above Salterns Lock used for boat moorings. The greater part of the upper reaches together with Southgate Basin however have been enthusiastically restored by the Chichester Canal Society, and small craft can now ply these waters, including public boat trips from Southgate Basin.

One can only hope that in future, connection to the sea can be remade, allowing craft once more to venture into Chichester's pretty little dock.

1. Chichester Canal

The Cathedral spire of Chichester must have made an excellent 'sight-line' for the navvies digging the final stretch to Southgate Basin. Sadly, and barely eighty years from its inception, it closed in 1906 commercially. In the photograph from around the time of closure, a small black hulled trading ketch can just be seen in front of the right hand of a pair of cottages. It must have been a Sunday, as well dressed Edwardian folk appear relaxing canalside. The iron frame of the gasometer confirms how important coal had been to the waterway.

2. Entrance to Southgate Basin →

A similar view in 2003, from a little closer to the Basin and the Canal Society's workboat is moored in exactly the same front of cottage berth. Otherwise most buildings are different, with the ever present Cathedral spire hiding behind the tree. Swans too, are still in residence.

3. Southgate Basin →

In this north-westerly view across the Basin, the tiny pusher-tug *Jupiter* is returning a pontoon with hydraulic excavator to its berth. Those 'navvies' of old surely could never have dreamed of such futuristic elimination of their back breaking toil. At the far end, the Canal Society's public trip boat *Egremont* is embarking passengers for a pleasant cruise down the canal.

4. Above Salterns Lock

Extending only about half a mile out of view, nature is
doing its level best to reclaim this lower disconnected
end of the Canal, where it joins the salt water of
Chichester Harbour. A splendidly diverse group of
house boats now line the tranquil lily covered reach,
above Salterns Lock. The smart motor yacht *Vere*, a
Dunkirk veteran, lies nearest to the lock gates. Built at
Gloucester in 1925 she has done well to reach 2004.

5. Salterns Lock →

With modern yachts visible beyond on the tideway, it
is not easy today to visualise commercial craft passing
this way, en route to Chichester, or barges for Arundel,
the Wey and Arun Canal, and London beyond. The
through traffic ran only from 1816 to 1850, by no
means a great success.

6. Dell Quay →

A small sprit sail barge lies aground at low tide with patient horses, carts and carters awaiting their turn to
load, in this idyllic 1900s scene. Absolutely typical of the period nationally in such local creeks, estuaries
and even open beaches, this was 'the way things had been done' for centuries, before the advent of proper
wharves and such facilities. The old barges capacity would have been in the region of 100 tons, the tiny carts,
perhaps a ton apiece. Labour, of course, was both plentiful and cheap, the hours long and hard, and all totally
wind and tide dependent.

7. Bosham Quay

A scene from around 1900 and somewhat devoid of activity, two small local trading vessels are loosely moored, awaiting the tide at Bosham. This was generally a busy spot for such craft, decent berths being here provided. Coal and farm related cargoes would have prevailed.

8. Bosham Quay (modern)

In this 1970s view the scene is reversed, the last commercial vessel has long since sailed and modern yachts are proliferating. The quay has evidently been re-piled accordingly - not a frequent consideration in earlier cargo handling days.

Emsworth and the J.D.Foster 'empire'

Situated five miles due north from the sea, at the head of the Emsworth Channel, this delightfull small town lies within the bounds of Chichester Harbour. Historically, shallow depths of water have doubtless affected the town's prosperity, although small coastal craft would have managed, spring tides had to be awaited for the deeper draughted traders.

Also, this criteria would have much influenced launch timings at Emsworth's once prolific shipyards, where in the 18th and 19th centuries many wooden sailing vessels came off the slipways. In general, local traders of between 20 and 50 reg.tons were constructed, together with a few larger ships up to about 180 tons. In terms of types the smaller were mainly cargo carrying cutters and ketches, and oyster smacks; the larger being schooners, brigantines and a barquentine, the *Sarah Amy*, 178 tons and built in 1874.

J.D.Foster & Co. built many of the Emsworth craft, and his ship building, timber, engineering and oyster dredging / processing business was indeed of some magnitude, employing many skilled tradesmen.

Unlike today, when oysters are considered something of a delicacy, they were in the 1800s quite a commonplace meal. By 1900 oysters and scallops had been worked almost out of existence on the inshore grounds. This was hardly surprising - the boom years had been in the mid 1800s - one contemporary record states that by this time, '20,000 tons of oysters annually were leaving Shoreham alone, by rail for the markets'. Such volumes were simply unsustainable. Larger oyster dredgers simply had to be developed to work new distant off-shore grounds mid-Channel, and in the North Sea.

J.D.Foster designed and built the *Echo* in 1901. She was unique in the U.K., a wooden hulled, ketch rigged vessel also steam powered, her dimensions were 80 grt; 110 ft. in length, 21ft. 6in. beam and with a maximum draught of 9ft. This last depth would preclude her from her own home port for much of the time. Fitted with a boiler and a 14 HP steam engine, *Echo* would employ both sails and screw propulsion when operating between nine and twelve oyster dredges, out on the deeper grounds. The boiler additionally provided steam for the dredging winches.

A 90 ton wet hold or 'well' full of sea water would sustain catch freshness for the duration of the voyage - which could be a few days duration, operating with a crew of eleven men. Between 1901 and her last working season in 1935-36, she would often work out of Newhaven's deepwater harbour, as a base for mid Channel dredging.

Briefly, *Echo* sailed as a yacht pre World War II, but by 1940 her sailing days, like the oyster trade, were over and sadly the old ship was 'torched' at Emsworth in the 1960s.

9. Emsworth Harbour

Not the sharpest of images, however this photograph gives a good indication of Emsworth's industrial and maritime importance in the 19th century. Ship building and owning, and the huge oyster fishing/ processing operation prevailed hereabouts. A group of sailing traders can be seen moored to the right, including topsail schooners and ketches.

10. CYMBA & RECOIL

Two of the smaller local vessels moored here are the barge *Recoil*, employed in collecting sand and gravel for the building trade and, nearest the camera, *Cymba*. J.D.Foster built this 23 reg.ton cutter in 1893 to join his own fleet of oyster smacks. An unusual feature is just discernible across the ship's transom - the letters 'J.D.F.' proudly carved thereon.

11. ECHO →
(the Queen of the Oyster Fleet)

By the time of this 1953 photograph, *Echo* had been out of use for many years and was sadly disintegrating. Her slender, lofty funnel is absent, and terminal decline has set in apace.

12. J.D.Foster- Memorial Plaque →

Set conspicuously by the waterside, this plaque honours Emsworth's once great industrialist.

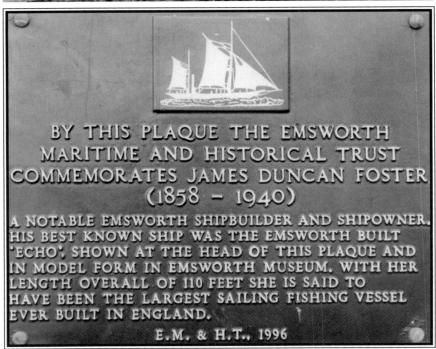

BY THIS PLAQUE THE EMSWORTH
MARITIME AND HISTORICAL TRUST
COMMEMORATES JAMES DUNCAN FOSTER
(1858 – 1940)
A NOTABLE EMSWORTH SHIPBUILDER AND SHIPOWNER.
HIS BEST KNOWN SHIP WAS THE EMSWORTH BUILT
'ECHO', SHOWN AT THE HEAD OF THIS PLAQUE AND
IN MODEL FORM IN EMSWORTH MUSEUM. WITH HER
LENGTH OVERALL OF 110 FEET SHE IS SAID TO
HAVE BEEN THE LARGEST SAILING FISHING VESSEL
EVER BUILT IN ENGLAND.
E.M. & H.T., 1996

Map No.2 Langstone Harbour

(1)   Langstone Rail & Road Bridges. Sidings to
       the former were the site of the short lived rail
       wagon ferry service to the Isle of Wight 1884-1888.
(2)   Salterns Jetty
(3)   Portsmouth to Hayling Island ferry.

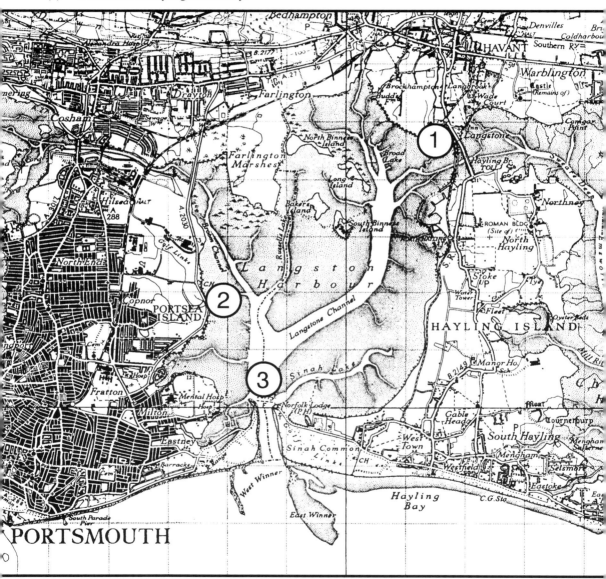

13.   PS   CARRIER - (the one and only Isle of Wight train ferry).

In 1872 the Isle of Wight Marine Transit Company agreed to provide the link cross-Solent between wharves at Langstone (Hayling Island branch line), and St.Helens Quay (Bembridge branch line), by way of a freight only rail ferry. From the outset it appears that very little good fortune befell the venture. Firstly, the specially constructed terminals at both locations were approached from the sea by way of twisting narrow shallow channels, navigable only at high tides. Secondly, the elderly paddle steamer selected to run the service had to remain in Scotland. This delay resulted from the Tay Bridge collapse disaster, *Carrier* continued to make her River Tay crossing for a few more years. Ultimately, in 1884 she came South to take up her new but spasmodic duties, across the Solent. Completed as early as 1858 for the North British Company, the steamer had two parallel standard gauge rail tracks, one gauge width apart. By way of a steam operated lifting cradle arrangement, up to fourteen simple goods wagons could be transferred to and from the wharf railheads, per voyage. At one end (forward) sets of buffers were fitted, thereby the ship always went stern first to the dock. *Carrier* had been built for river crossings, and this factor plus her age, lack of flexibility, and the exposed nature of the crossing to the Isle of Wight, together with those twisting channels, did not constitute a recipe for success. Within four years the service ceased and after a period in lay-up, Swedish owners managed to squeeze a few more years out of the old ship. Langstone wharves siltation problem worsened and they too closed by about 1900. On the Island side, St.Helens Quays were kept open to traffic only after a major dredging programme in Bembridge's channels. The PS CARRIER was built at Greenock, in 1858 and was 243 grt. 124ft loa. by 24ft 6in. br. by 8ft. 6in. draught. The photograph, courtesy of the National Maritime Museum is thought to have been taken at Granton, Scotland before the voyage to the Solent area. A model and detailed information on this fascinating but short lived operation may be seen in the Bembridge Heritage Centre, Isle of Wight.

14. Old Ferry Dock, Langstone.

The view northwards in 2004 towards Havant shows a surprisingly large number of wooden pile stumps remaining. These once formed the end of the old wharf tramway siding.

15. Hayling Island Rail Bridge (remains)

From the spot described in 14; the scene southwards towards Hayling Island shows the line of the railway curving to the right in the distance. The dark block visible is the base remains of the old swingbridge over the barge channel. British Railways closed this line in 1963; bridge demolition occurred in 1966.

Map No.2.1 Langstone Wharves

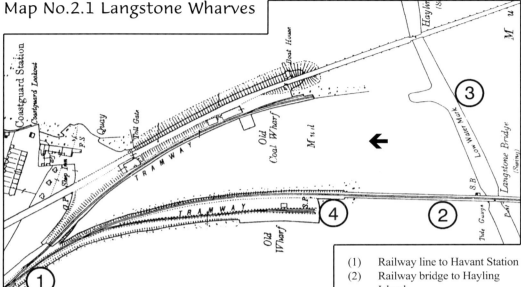

(1) Railway line to Havant Station
(2) Railway bridge to Hayling Island.
(3) Old barge channel north of Hayling Island - part of the route for the Portsmouth to Arundel and London canal traffic.
(4) The site of the 1884-1888 rail truck steamer berth for *PS Carrier*.

16. EOLUS

Built as late as 1949, right at the end of wooden ship construction in Sweden, this vessel had originally been configured as an auxiliary powered, sailing cargo ship. Of 262grt 315dwt the 109ft. loa *Eolus* continued to carry cargo until the 1960s. By 1974 she had been prepared for a 'round the World' venture, re-rigged as a barquentine and renamed '*Black Pearl*'. Various setbacks seem to have beset her subsequent career and she was last reported 'set in concrete' in Malta, by 1982. In the 1974 photograph, still as *Eolus* she lays at Salterns Jetty on the west side of Langstone harbour, soon to commence her epic trip.

17. Hayling Ferry (1900)

A group of laden spritsail coasting barges lie off the Ferry. This short crossing saves a thirteen mile road trip for intending foot passengers.

18. Hayling Ferry (modern)

Little appears to have changed in this 2004 scene. A modern ferry plies the route at this idyllic Langstone Harbour entrance crossing. Yachts replace sailing barges, hereabouts.

Map No.3 Portsmouth Harbour

(1)   Camber Docks, Portsmouth's original commercial trading heart.
(2)   Railway Station and Jetty for IOW foot passenger ferry traffic, opened 1876.
(3)   Landport. Old shipyards and gasworks. Now cross - Channel ferry and commercial port.
(4)   Fareham Creek and Quays.
(5)   Gosport ferry terminal.

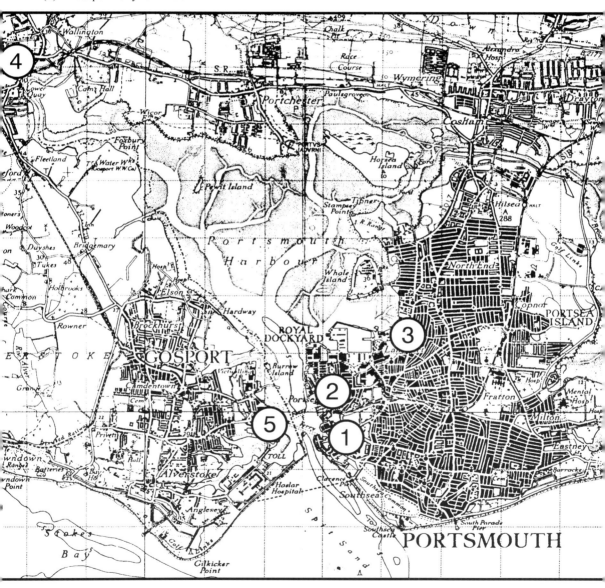

19. Gosport Slipway

HMS Victory lies at her mooring in this busy scene. It was not until 1922 that the 1778 built ship entered her present drydock resting place. A local trading ketch, with boat trailing astern is setting off under gaff mainsail, whilst cross harbour steam launches abound. The one off the slipway is the 1893 built, 47 grt *Prince*, often otherwise engaged in the excursion trade to the Beaulieu River at this period. She was a member of the Gosport and Portsea Watermans Steam Launch Company fleet. The photograph is from about 1900.

20. Portsmouth to Gosport Terminal →

Another steam launch, *Vesta II*, Millwall built in 1909, lies alongside the Harbour Station pontoon. The curved branch railway connection to HM Dockyard seems to be employed as a carriage siding on this occasion. Special trains for Royals and visiting foreign dignitaries mostly journeyed this way, the connection to the railway main line being at the end of Portsmouth Harbour station's platform one. This scene dates from about 1910. *Vesta II* lasted a very long time-she later operated at Southampton in the 1960s and 1970s, sailing as *Southampton Belle*, converted to diesel power.

21. Gosport Chain Ferry

A service for wheeled traffic operated from the foot of Broad Street, Old Portsmouth to Gosport from 1840 to 1959. The ferries were of a curious double-ended, double- sided design, and steam driven until the end. For vehicular traffic they eliminated a journey of sixteen miles by road. Similarly, the little steam launches saved about an hours trip. With ever increasing harbour traffic, the old chain ferry, by its very nature ponderous in movement, was discontinued. The scene dates from around 1920.

22. PS DUCHESS OF FIFE

A product of Clydebank Engineering Ltd; this 1899 built 400 grt steamer typifies the larger paddler of the day. With plenty of closed in accommodation for year round ferry services, she also had good deck space for those all important excursions. Indeed, paddle steamer design would alter little subsequently, thereafter.*Duchess of Fife* ran for the joint LB&SC Railway and L&SW Railway services until formation of the Southern Railway in 1923. She was scrapped in 1929. The history of this service to Ryde goes back to 1814 when paddlers ran for the Portsmouth and Ryde Steam Packet Company from Southsea to Ryde's newly opened pier. It was not until 1873 that the Admiralty deemed Portsmouth Naval Base secure enough to permit construction of the railway onwards from Portsmouth & Southsea, to the Harbour Station. By 1879 the railway companies had absorbed all earlier ferry operators on this route to the Isle of Wight.

As a brief 'aside'-- Great Grandmother, en route from the IOW to Sussex, blind and of very advanced years, was once craned ashore complete with wheelchair, ex steamer at Portsmouth Harbour Station. Quite what the old lady made of this form of disembarkation went unrecorded!

23. SL VADNE →

Locally built by Vospers in 1939 the increasing size of the 'Gosport' ferries is evident in this c1950 photograph. Workers and their cycles may be seen on the foredeck as the vessel approaches her destination, and where can you put a steaming light on a mastless ferry?- below the steam whistle on the funnel, of course!

24. MV SHANKLIN →

In 1946 the Southern Railway ordered replacement ferries for those paddle steamers lost during the War. In a revolutionary move, three motor ferries of 200 ft.loa and 46ft.br., capable of carrying up to 1,400 passengers would begin to supersede the few faithful paddlers still in service. At 830 grt (later re-measured at 965 grt), the new *Southsea*, *Brading* and *Shanklin* were to be Sulzer engine powered. They entered service between 1948 and 1951 under British Railways nationalised auspices. For many years they continued to run with the last of the 1930s paddlers - *Whippingham*, *Ryde* and *Sandown*, on the Ryde service and local excursions. In this early view of Shanklin, although radar fitted, she has yet to receive a mainmast required later by SOLAS Navigation Light Rules - to display a second masthead steaming light for a vessel over 150ft. in length. In 1980 *Shanklin* was sold, renamed *Prince Ivanhoe* and intended as an operating consort for *PS Waverley* to help fund raising. Sadly, she struck rocks in 1981 along the South Wales coast, and was a total loss.

25. Broad Street Slipway (1) & MV WOOTTON

Pre 1927, IOW bound carriages / livestock / motor vehicles had to make the journey from this location by way of 'tow-boats' and steam tugs. The recently formed Southern Railway soon spotted the potential for specialised vehicular ferries for this route. The small double ended motor ferries *Fishbourne*, *Wootton* and *Hilsea* entered service in 1927/8, running to a new purpose-built slipway at Fishbourne, on the Island's Wootton Creek. Once up and running, this whole new roll-on, roll-off concept steadily expanded, although freight traffic generally meant light lorries and vans. In fact, it was not until the 1950s that a slightly larger second generation of motor ferries materialised, on this route. This particular 1950s photograph nicely captures the rudimentary nature of the operation. In the background looms the bulk of Portsmouth's coal fired power station, with the steam collier *Pompey Light* unloading by grab crane, in her own specially provided 'single ship' dock. *Fishbourne*, *Wootton* and *Hilsea*, each of 149 grt could manage sixteen cars apiece, or less with some commercial vehicles onboard. The journey time to Fishbourne was around 50 minutes at 8kts. As the access ramp arrangements can clearly be seen , it seems an appropriate moment to interject another brief 'aside'.

The author's Father boldly drove his brand new BSA three wheeler sports car to the Island in 1928. Apparently it was the custom at Broad Street to place a couple of timbers up against the lip of the ferry's ramp, to ease the passage of wheels onto the ferry. The supervisor on this occasion, after a little head scratching, summoned a third timber to be centrally placed—he had not encountered a 'car-sized' vehicle previously, that had but one centrally placed rear wheel - boarding progressed smoothly.

26. SS POMPEY POWER →

Portsmouth Corporation wisely decided in 1946 to ensure coal deliveries locally by ordering two steam colliers of their own. The well equipped ships came from the Sunderland shipyard of S.P.Austin & Co., duly entering service in 1949. *Pompey Power* 1,428 grt 1,780 dwt actually displayed the Corporation's colours on her funnel, for one voyage. The nationalisation of the country's electricity industry then ensued, and all such ships were coordinated under the BEA (British Electricity Authority) logo. Some years later this altered to CEA (Central Electricity Authority), the ships' funnels again reflecting the change. In 1958 the letters were omitted entirely, leaving black topped, red funnels. *Pompey Power*, being deemed surplus to coal demand requirements in 1960, went to Norweigian owners. *Pompey Light* continued alone until 1960, going for scrap in a Belgium yard. The present (1982) Gun Wharf I.O.W. car ferry terminal resides on the old power station site.

27. MV HAMEN (ex. POMPEY POWER)

A well found ship, a mere eleven years old obviously has potentially another ten or twenty years trading life ahead. *Pompey Power's* new Norweigian owners indeed made the most of a sound hull. She was converted into a very useful general trader. The steam engine went in favour of a more economical diesel, hatches were modified and new masts, cargo derricks and winches fitted, together with a more appropriate shortened funnel. Renamed *Hamen*, the ship continued often to trade to the U.K. with timber cargoes, returning with coal. The ship is seen here in early 1960s guise.

28. SS FLATHOUSE

Portsmouth's gasworks was situated to the north east of the Naval Dockyard at Flathouse Quay, which today, with Albert Johnson Quay form the current commercial shipping facility. The well known steam coaster company, Stephenson Clarke, ordered *Flathouse* in 1931. Another Sunderland built, ship she measured 1,559 grt 2,255 dwt and then set about supplying gas making coal to the port for the next thirty years, going for scrap in 1961.

29. MV ORSELINA →

This smart but unremarkable little motor coaster had already put in twenty years trading for Robert Rix of Hull. Dutch built in 1938 and of 258 grt she comes from a time when efficient motor coasters were gaining the upper hand, and beginning to edge out the smaller steam coasters. By 1960, *Ebbrix*, now renamed *Orselina* was operating on various routes to the Channel Islands for Commodore Shipping. A very far cry from the large vehicular ferries on that route today.

30. Camber Dock / MV STADT ESSEN

This is the reverse view to no.25, towards Broad Street Slipway, and shows three 'modern' motor coasters working cargo in Camber Dock, towards the end of its major cargo handling days. Portsmouth's sea borne commerce had passed this way for centuries. In the 1950s Dutch and German motor coasters, often 500 tonners, held sway in many of the Northern European trades. In the scene from around 1959, one is visible with tug and barge alongside, *Stadt Essen* of Rendsburg, and the Dutchman, *Henriette B.*, are also present. The latter is moored approximately where cars are marshalled at Gun Wharf for the IOW ferry, today.

31. MV VITA

Thousands who daily traversed the Portsmouth to Gosport route will doubtless remember this little ferry built by Camper and Nicholsons, in 1960. Diesel power was replacing steam at this time and the 68 grt *Vita* helped maintain the service until 1974 when she moved to the Thames for further work. Amazingly, at forty four years of age, and looking smart in a bright red livery, the little ship is seen here at Tower Pier in 2004. Her old running mate *Ferry Queen* of 1959 is similarly still engaged.

32. Gun Wharf (HMS Vernon) →

Still much used by the Navy in 1978, there are various landing craft and a 'Ton' class minesweeper visible at the base in this scene. Also, still piercing the distant skyline are the two Portsmouth power station chimneys - a few years from demolition. The vista here has totally altered in the last two decades; now the massive Gun Wharf Quays shopping, office, residential development and marina facility, dominate. Just a few feet out of shot to the left, the Millenium Tower, approached completion in 2004.

33. Broad Street's second Slipway →

Truck traffic expansion both in size and numbers saw the introduction of second generation car ferries to Fishbourne around 1960. The terminals were upgraded accordingly. In this 1967 photograph, the quayside visible between the trailer roof and coaster stern, would duly become the location for the next move in 1982, to the present Gun Wharf site.

34. ROYALIST and MV SHANKLIN

Groves and Gutteridge of Cowes built the delightful little steel hulled brig *Royalist*, 110 tons, in 1971 as a sail training ship. In this mid 1970s Portsmouth entrance scene, some Cadets are aloft to unfurl sail, whilst the ship motors out to sea. Passing inwards *Shanklin* heads for the Harbour Station, and is just coming abeam of the green crane on Point Wharf. Daily cargo barges ran from this exposed wharf to the Isle of Wight, courtesy of British Road Services for many years. The service ceased about 1975. Beyond *Shanklin* one of the second generation, 300 ton car ferries lies at the mooring pontoon. *HMS Victory's* mainmast was evidently receiving attention - being 'top-mastless', at this time.

35. MV EL MANSOOR SAAIL →

The new, and third car ferry location has materialised at Gun Wharf by the time of this 1984 view. On the opposite quay, a 1,599 grt 1976 built Moroccan registered, refrigerated cargo ship is berthed. Visitations to Camber Dock by large craft other than the IOW car ferries were becoming rarer by this time. In due course the refrigerated trades moved north of the Dockyard, to a home capable of receiving much larger, ocean going vessels.

36. MV ST.CATHERINE →

Under early Sealink livery, this 2,036 grt ferry entered service in 1983. Representing a big increase in ship size with a capacity for 142 cars and a faster service speed, the class of four vessels, although double ended were more conventional in layout, with a forward bridge and central funnel. The vehicle 'drive-through' concept achieved by always 'turning-ship' when off the terminals, unlike the earlier types. Also passenger capacity increased to 1,000, as coaches on day trips were becoming big business for the Island. As the ship heads into Portsmouth, the last remnant of red brick power station paraphernalia, had yet to be demolished, and can be seen over the stern ramp. By 1984 Sealink had been de-nationalised, thence forming part of Sea Containers, Ltd.

37. Portsmouth Shipping

A 2002 evening sunshine scene off the Harbour Station. On the mooring pontoon can be seen one of the Saint class car ferries in Wightlink livery, plus one of the Company's Fastcats introduced in 1986, to modernise the Ryde Pier passenger service. *Our Lady Pamela* and *Our Lady Patricia*, 313 grt each, were built in Tasmania and would cut the cross-Solent trip down to fifteen minutes, thus allowing retirement of the 1948 built *Southsea* class. Inboard, on the mooring is the bunkering tanker *Jaynee W*, 1,689 grt of 1986. Above the group, *Warrior* and *Victory's* masts rise loftily. Far distant left, the Channel Islands container ship *Huelin Despatch*, 1,892 grt of 1978 has just left the commercial port for home.

38. MV ST.CLARE →

Caught awaiting the outgoing sailing to clear the berth, the additional height of this latest vessel is much apparent. This has enabled the configuration of a permanent upper car deck, impossible in the earlier 'Saint' class vessels, where of necessity such car decks had to be hydraulically positioned, on demand. At some 5,000 grt the 2001 Polish built *St.Clare*, apart from her greater size, does represent a return to the true double ended concept - eliminating 'turning ship' at voyage ends.

39. MV ST.CLARE at Gun Wharf Terminal →

This 2003 view makes an interesting comparison to no.25 Broad Street Old Slipway photo, with *Wootton* unloading. In fact the concrete slipway is the only constant in the entire scene. *St.Clare* is at the loading berth whilst an earlier 'Saint' lies at the lay-by berth beyond. Other than the half hourly ferry movements hereabouts, Camber Dock system now handles a variety of small craft such as tugs, fishing vessels, and pilot launches.

40. MVs ST.HELEN and MARINE VENTURE

The red hulled visitor in this 2003 photograph is the survey ship *Marine Venture* of Grimsby. Note beyond, the huge increase in truck / trailer traffic upon which the Isle of Wight, and indeed the whole Nation now depend. Portsmouth Cathedral looks on, as all about changes.

41. MV LOYAL WATCHER →

Once a member of a large class of Royal Naval Fleet tenders, *Loyal Watcher* like many of her contemporaries from the 1970s, has joined the commercial world. In original form these little ships provided small cargo / stores carriage / personnel conveyance / and training roles. In 'civvy street' many have made ideal workboats for surveying, exploration and minor salvage jobs. This 2004 photo is specially included as it clearly shows the second Broad Street Slipway, in use up to 1982. Vehicles intending to board the Fishbourne ferry had to turn 180 degrees out of the car park, to achieve their aim.

42. MT WHITSPRAY →

The 1969 built, 899 grt coastal tanker is seen here in 2003 bunkering a Naval vessel. *Whitspray* had started her trading life as *Bristolian*. In the background one each of P&O and Brittany Ferries' cross-Channel superferries, can be seen lying at their respective Continental Ferry Port, roll-on, roll-off berths.

43. Continental Ferry Port

To the right of the cross - Channel ships, two vessels of the Dutch 'Seatrade' Company fleet of Groningen, may be seen unloading at Albert Johnson and Flathouse Quays. These berths now provide a specialist service to the Worldwide perishable produce trade. Fast refrigerated cargo ships are frequent callers where once the gasworks colliers unloaded, and in earlier times at Landport, wooden sailing cargo ships were built and owned in the 1800s.

44. Fareham Quay

In the most north-westerly corner of Portsmouth Harbour lies Fareham Creek, leading to the town of that name. In this scene from about 1900, local ketch barge traffic is much evident, with sand, grain and coal cargoes likely to be prevalent. The nearest old gaff rigged barge, minus a topmast, looks to be well laden with just one such commodity. Tidal considerations, especially at the top end of winding creeks, ruled the day as ever, in such locations.

45. MB BAT at Fareham Quay

A variety of hulls (and fifties motor cars) pose in front of the Fareham Flour Mill Company premises in around 1960, each well outnumbered by a flotilla of swans. The *Bat*, whose bow is clearly visible, was an interesting old motor barge, that had been engaged in cross-Solent trade for Pickfords, for decades. Dutch built in 1912 and of 74 grt she would have carried about 100 tons of whatever there was on offer, into any of the region's smallest rivers and creeks.

46. Fareham Ballast Quay

Still occasionally visited by the smaller sand and ballast carriers in 2003, like the majority of local creeks today, Fareham relies on the yachting industry. Gone are the flour mills and hubbub of visiting barge traffic, once the lifeblood for many a town at the top end of a navigable creek.

Map No.4 Southampton Water
Calshot Point, River Hamble etc.

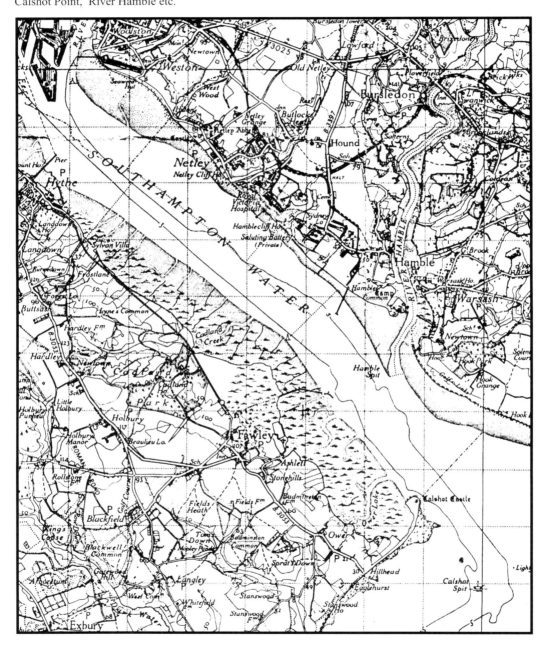

Map No.5 Southampton Docks and Rivers to Eling

(1)   Itchen Ferry and today's Itchen Bridge.

(2)   Driver's Wharf, Northam Bridge.

(3)   Town Quay, Cowes Ferry, etc.

(4)   Eling Creek and Quays.

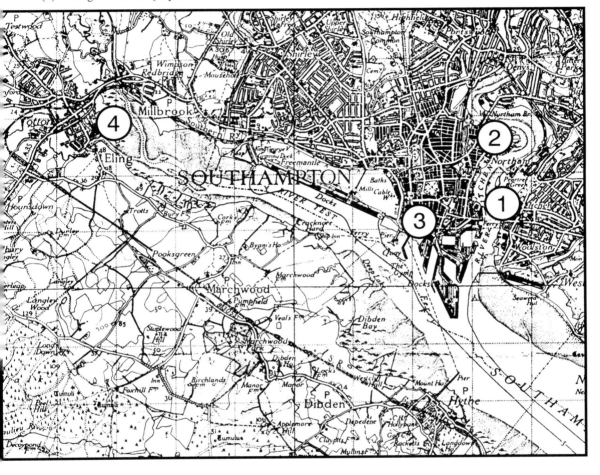

47. ROSIE at Northam Bridge

The rivers and creeks of Southampton Water had witnessed centuries of trade before the construction of the first 'modern' dock, the 'outer' dock in 1843. One such ancient trading area was the River Itchen. This delightful Victorian photograph from 1889 shows the scene immediately below Northam Bridge, where the 1886 Littlehampton built ketch *Rosie*, 78 reg tons is working cargo by way of a wharfside hand crane. Just visible to the left is the stern of another sailing trader in the small, cut-in dock. Beyond lies the 1799 to 1889 timber trestle bridge, replaced at that time by an iron structure. This in turn gave way to the present 1954 concrete bridge.

48. MV SOUTHSEA (below Northam Bridge)

One hundred and fifty years later, in 2004 the sad form of the ex Portsmouth to Ryde ferry *Southsea* lies about where *Rosie* had been moored. Despite some well intentioned preservation ideas coming and going, the old ship continues to deteriorate, and the scene is somehow completed by the mountain of scrap metal piled on the quayside, awaiting export.

49. Sail on the Itchen

A selection of wooden barques lay moored after discharging their cargoes on the Itchen in the 1880s. Steam had yet to replace sail in many trades. It is likely that these old timers had brought Baltic timber. Neatly moored in line, in the foreground are half a dozen local craft known as Itchen ferry punts. They were unique to the area and would be used for fishing, or, as general runabouts. Rigged as gaff cutters, a number of these sturdy little boats survive to this day, as yachts.

50. Itchen Floating Bridge

With further square riggers out in the River, a contingent of very well dressed ladies and children are disembarking from Southampton Corporation's No.7 'guided' steam ferry in 1900. This service from the Southampton side to Woolston, across the Itchen, started in 1836, and ran until the completion of the high level concrete bridge structure of recent decades. Unlike the Portsmouth to Gosport chain ferry, these craft had a central vehicle deck, with passenger accommodation each side.

51. MV DONALD REDFORD →

A familiar sight around the Solent, the 1981 built 681 grt *Donald Redford* entered service as a grab crane dredger in the Mersey area. Later converted to the suction arm system, the ship then entered the sea dredged aggregates trade to the building industry. Photographed in 2004 at Woolston, the discharge is proceeding in the conventional shore crane way.

52. Upriver from the Itchen Bridge →

The River Itchen still witnesses considerable small craft activity between Itchen and Northam Bridges, with visiting coasters, tugs, dredgers and work craft. The striking roof structure of St.Mary's Football Stadium is clearly visible on the Southampton bank of the river.

53. Vosper Thorneycroft's Shipyard (closed)

In 2004 the great doors were closed and silence has fallen where decades of naval and merchant ship building took place. Demolition was imminent. However, this has in part been off-set by expansion at the Portsmouth Naval Base.

54. ST ATTUNITY →

One of a series of tiny coastal tankers built at the very end of World War II, the 143 grt *Attunity*, from 1945 is seen here just off the mouth of the Itchen River. She had found her way along with several sister vessels into F.T.Everards' huge coastal fleet. Powered by a two cylinder steam engine, she was quite capable of coastwise trips to the smallest distribution facilities, and no doubt, bunkered many a larger vessel. In the background a group of local 'Esso' bunkering tankers can be seen moored to the pier. Also visible far left are naval vessels afloat at the Woolston Shipyard in rather happier, more productive times. *Attunity* was later 'motorised' and renamed *Ernie Spearing* in 1967, operating as a water carrier. She survives to this day in the North East, as *Abercraig*.

55. PS FRESHWATER (in lay-up) →

Samuel White's, Cowes Shipyard built the pretty little paddle steamer *Freshwater* for the Southern Railway in 1927. She operated on the Lymington to Yarmouth route until being finally made redundant by the car ferries in the 1950s. In this 1958 photograph and still looking very smart, the ship is in lay-up at Southampton's Inner Dock, in front of the massive L&SWRailway warehouse of 1897. This dock was in-filled in 1977. After briefly operating as *Swanage Queen*, then *Sussex Queen*, she went for scrap in the early 1960s - rather a shame, as with such modest dimensions a good candidate for preservation had been lost.

56. MV ASHLEIGH-R at Ocean Village

The once bustling Outer Dock, dating from 1843, now reflects a major change in utilisation. Designer homes, offices and plush yachts have replaced the commerce of old, and all its trappings, in this 2004 photograph.

57. Hythe Ferry and MV ARCO SEVERN →

Arriving at Southampton on her routine crossing from Hythe, is a catamaran-hulled motor ferry delightfully named *Great Expectations*. With the older *Hotspur IV* as running mate, the two craft maintain the ancient link across Southampton Water to the New Forest side. This is a busy commuter route, saving about ten miles by road. In the background the 1974 built suction dredger *Arco Severn*, 1,915 grt is out of service in this 2004 scene.

58. PS SOUTHAMPTON at Royal Pier →

Two early units of Red Funnel's fleet await the day's passengers around 1896, for the run to Cowes. Historically, paddle steamers had been at work on this route since 1836. By 1861, the Southampton, Isle of Wight and South Coast Royal Mail Steam Packet Company Limited who thankfully, soon became known simply as Red Funnel, were running paddlers up to about 100 tons size. In 1872 *PS Southampton* had entered service. With a length of 150ft.and a service speed of twelve knots, she could carry 272 passengers. After thirty years on the Cowes run she briefly operated from Newhaven in 1902, but later ended her career as *St.Eilian* on the North Wales coast, scrapping in 1915.

59. PS LORD ELGIN (as passenger ship)

Few would have imagined this ship's long term prospects at her 1875 launch. The 198 grt iron hulled vessel was just another typical excursion steamer of the mid Victorian period. Initially, she operated in the Bournemouth area, but came into Red Funnel hands in 1908. In 1910 a major transformation occurred as the old ship was stripped of her passenger accommodation facilities, given a single mast, derrick and winch on the afterdeck, and put into service as a cargo ship on the Southampton to Cowes run. She became something of a legend locally, making a daily cross-Solent run excepting Sundays, with whatever cargo might be on offer. Herds of farm animals were a speciality. By the 1950s, with modern vehicle ferries coming into service, *Lord Elgin* was retired, going for scrap locally in 1955, seventy nine years from launching.

60. PS LORD ELGIN → (as cargo ship)

With the later addition of a peculiar 'V'- shaped wooden wheelhouse, this 1950s aerial view shows the old steamer plodding across the Solent, in her final guise - the very last sea-going British cargo paddle steamer.

61. SS ISLE OF JERSEY →

Together with sister ships *Isle of Guernsey* and *Isle of Sark*, these 1930s built steam turbine powered ships served on the Channel Islands and France passenger ferry runs until the route closed in 1964. This terminated over one hundred years of railway passenger services, cross - Channel from Southampton. In the 1950s photograph a good number of passengers appear to be onboard, and to afford a little extra weather protection, the sides of the poop deck house have been canvassed. At a little over 2,000 grt apiece, this class were of a typical size of the day.

62. ST ATTENDANT

This old workhorse dates from 1914 when she was built by, and for the Navy at Chatham Dockyard. Of 999 grt after forty years Naval work she converted from dry cargo to tanker operation, and would thence give several more years service to new owner, Hemsley, Bell Ltd. Ships with bridges perched right forward are common enough today, but in 1914 quite rare except for the Navy, who had a number of oilers built to this layout. The photograph dates from the mid 1950s.

63. SS DEAL →

Although an infrequent performer on Southampton's railway cargo services to the Continent, this ship represents a class of steamers, similarly engaged. At 839 grt the 1928 built *Deal* and her consorts carried all manner of general cargo. They also had to cope with the frenetic seasonal bursts of trade such as the Channel Island tomato and potato liftings. A few of these ships were later replaced by motor ships, but in the end all succumbed to container / trailer and roll-on, roll-off systems. The photograph dates from the early 1950s.

64. MV SAND DIVER →

With post World War II reconstruction and general growth, the building trade needed more sand and ballast. Offshore deposits in relatively shallow water became vital to the maintenance of supplies. A number of small motor cargo ships were specially converted for this operation. The 379 grt *Empire Farrier* of 1944 converted in 1953. The long dredging suction pipe can be clearly seen stowed on the starboard side, as she sets off for another load, under South Coast Shipping's colours.

65. SS SHIELDHALL

A ship that 'fate has smiled upon' surely applies to this 1955-built twin screw steamer, of 1,792 grt Glasgow Corporation ordered her for the City's sewage sludge disposal operation, from Lobnitz and Co.'s, Renfrew yard. She comes from the very end of reciprocating engined ship construction, the last steam colliers and trawlers also appeared at about this time. *Shieldhall's* unusual secondary function was the carriage of 'excursion' passengers down the River Clyde to sea. At the end of 1976 she was superseded by a modern motor ship, and the scrapyard looked likely. However, in 1977 Southern Water purchased the ship, up-graded her, and began to operate from Southampton in 1980. When European directives finally barred the disposal of sludge at sea, *Shieldhall* was withdrawn again in 1985. The ship is again fully operational under preservation by the Solent Steam Packet Company, and makes a number of local cruises each year. Good fortune indeed for a vessel originally designed for such a fundamental freight. In this 2002 scene she is steaming down Southampton Water.

66. MT HUMBER STAR →

Motoring steadily past Southampton Docks in 2002 is the esturial type motor tank barge *Humber Star*, 274 grt and originally named *Wade Stone* in 1969 for Cory Tank Craft. The type are designed for 'under the bridges' service such as on the Thames, but are capable of 'sheltered' estuary voyages.

67. MT WHITCHALLENGER →

At work here in Southampton Water in 2004 is the almost new 3,114 grt *Whitchallenger*, built in 2002. Engaged in bunkering larger ships, and designed for coastal voyages, the ship clearly shows the evolutionary design of lifeboats. A single, totally enclosed, stern fitted, gravity launched and gantry lifted boat, replaces the more traditional port and starboard davit type installations. A smaller crane operated rescue boat can be employed for emergencies, other than abandonment. The ship is Isle of Man registered and part of a large fleet run by Whitaker Ltd., of Hull. Passing by is the grey form of the deck barge, *MTB Blade Runner Two* en route to the River Medina.

68. MV ROUSTEL

Heading towards Southampton Docks, with Hamble in the background in this 2002 photograph is the 1978 built, 892 grt coaster *Roustel*. She has also traded under the name *Skellig Rock*.

69. MV BOISTEROUS →

Once a member of the Crescent Shipping fleet, the 664 grt 1983 built ship has forsaken her previous owner's reddish brown hull colour, for pale green. With minimal fuss and brush strokes the original name of *Boisterence* is less altered. Dry cargo coasters of about 1,000 tons dwt are becoming quite a rarity now in the coastal trades. In the background can be seen the Warsash, School of Navigation, at the mouth of the Hamble River, in this 2004 scene.

70. BESSIE →

Thames and Medway type sailing barges were equally well suited to the shallower, winding creeks of the Solent. Here in 1912, the Rochester built *Bessie*, dating from the 1880s, makes an ideal regatta boat for the local event at Eling Creek. Dressed overall and with a good number of folk aboard, the old barge and her crew are at least briefly away from the daily grind of coal, grain, sand, bricks or cement - the customary abrasive freights of the day, requiring manual labour.

71. Eling Wharves (post World War II)

This small historic haven at the upper limit of navigation on the River Test, had seen ship building in earlier times. More recently, much Baltic timber arrived for importers Burt, Bolton and Heywood Ltd; also Fisons had a fertiliser depot adjacent to the Quay. The tide is out in this early 1950s photograph, leaving a small Dutch or German motor coaster, sitting on the mud to complete discharge. Today, aggregates are still handled locally.

72. Eling Creek →

In this 2004 view, a giant stack of 40 ft. containers replaces 'all that has gone before'. Eling's proximity to Southampton's vast container terminal, across the water, is all too apparent. Yachts now line the local quays where barges and small coasters once served the mills, or brought coal.

73. Eling Tide Mill →

With its quaint narrow toll bridge and tide mill perched to catch the outgoing stream for power, this is today a tranquil spot, yet so close to modern industry. The Eling Heritage Centre is housed in the lower part of the building on the right of this 2004 photograph, and is a must for historians and tourists, alike.

Map No.6 Beaulieu River
(1) Bucklers Hard

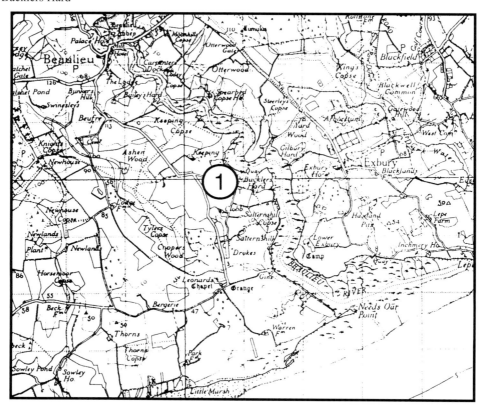

74. Off Bucklers Hard

The present placid waters of the Beaulieu River once formed a major haven of commerce. In the 1700s the West Indies sugar trade passed this way, and local ship builders sent many a stout wooden warship down the slipways, in Nelson's Navy times. The early 20th century saw an influx of tourists, often arriving from the Portsmouth area in little steam launches, such as the one passing a solitary yacht in this 1900s scene. Sixty years ago the river was again thronged with craft mustering for the D-Day landings. Today, tourism and yachting prevail.

75. Bucklers Hard

A group of three of those little steamers simmer at the pier whilst their passengers experience the rustic delights on offer, hereabouts. This was indeed a most popular destination for the Portsmouth and Gosport boats.

76. SL DUKE OF YORK

At 56 tons, Gosport built and owned, this 1900 built steamer has just left Bucklers Hard for the return leg, and appears very lightly laden in this 1910 scene. Today, a modern passenger vessel, the *Swiftsure* plies the River, affording tourists a local scenic cruise.

77. SY CAROLA

In this 1970s scene the private Victorian steam yacht *Carola* lies at Bucklers Hard wharf, beyond the simple Scotch derrick crane. Of 1898 vintage and 40 grt she was built at Bowling, Scotland and is still in existence.

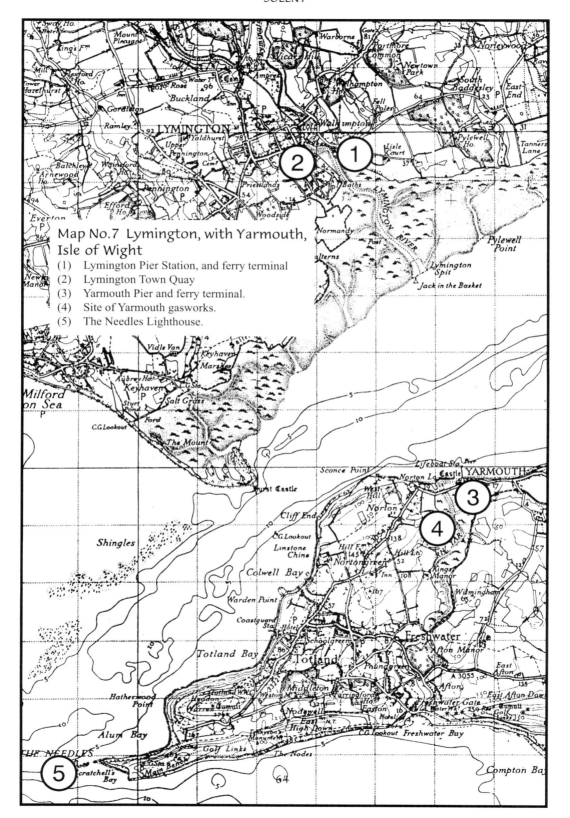

Map No.7 Lymington, with Yarmouth,
Isle of Wight

(1) Lymington Pier Station, and ferry terminal
(2) Lymington Town Quay
(3) Yarmouth Pier and ferry terminal.
(4) Site of Yarmouth gasworks.
(5) The Needles Lighthouse.

78. PS SOLENT

In 1858 the Lymington Railway Company's branch line from Brockenhurst reached Lymington Town. 'Tow-boats' had been in use since 1836, transporting goods to and from Yarmouth, the nearest Island port to the Mainland. By 1884 the London and South Western Railway Company, now in charge, had constructed Lymington Pier and Station, half a mile down river from the town, and on the opposite bank. This enabled the paddle steamers to come and go at pretty much all states of the tide - regular service timetables had arrived. The 'tow-boat' service for goods and vehicles would however continue for another fifty years, these barge-like vessels trailing astern of the steamers or tugs, for the crossing. The early paddlers were very rudimentary in design, but by 1902 when *Solent*, 161 grt entered service, more generous covered accommodation materialised. In this early photograph the paddler is just approaching the pier. *Solent* helped maintain local services throughout the Second World War, being finally withdrawn from service in 1948.

79. Lymington Pier and Station

Still appearing pristine around 1910, the curve of the railway embankment leads the eye round to the neat signal box and station, where *PS Solent* awaits the 'off' for Yarmouth. Note apart from the one little white yacht, the Lymington River seems devoid of other craft.

80. SS SLATEFORD, SS ROYAL FIRTH, and MYRTLE

Days of high industry are seen here at Lymington Quay around 1923. The photograph, although from a rare and damaged original, shows three clearly identifiable craft. From left to right: *Slateford*, 355 grt built in 1903; and *Royal Firth*, 411 grt built in 1921 are both typical small steam coasters of the period. The former belonged to Ford Shipping; the latter to Gillie and Blair. Alongside *Royal Firth*, the local trading ketch *Myrtle* of 45 reg.tons, and built at Emsworth in 1898 is moored. Her owners were the well known Fraser and White Company, of Portsmouth. Coal for the local utilities and domestic use probably featured high on the agenda for all three vessels. The cross river ferryman has but a single fare to convey.

81. PS FRESHWATER (in service) →

A few wooden sailing boats witness the outward passage of the lightly loaded *Freshwater*, seen here in the 1930s, Southern Railway era. Paddlers on the Lymington River sometimes set a small sail on the forestay, to aid turning in the restricted area off the Pier.

82. Lymington Town Quay and MB XXXX →

Some motor cruisers lie off the Quay in 1952. Alongside, the Mew, Langton Brewery Company's barge *XXXX* from Newport, IOW is moored at their Lymington depot. Built at Cowes in 1948, she bore this unusual beer strength name long before it became popular from the Antipodean quarter .

Note: A deviation from the Mainland to Yarmouth IOW follows, in line with Map No.7 coverage.

83. Yarmouth Harbour

The Castle, quay and wooden pier are unchanging, but the harbour was certainly in dire need of a dredge about 1908. The few yachts of the time took up little mooring space. A black hulled cutter, the *Pilot*, of 1834, 18 tons and built at Lymington, but owned in Yarmouth, sits barely afloat. Offshore, beyond the 1876 pier a white hulled topsail schooner 'ghosts' along.

84. Yarmouth Quay in bleak mid-winter →

With a couple of local trading ketches and three 'tow-boats' alongside, humans appear to have retreated indoors for warmth. The distant mud flats and salt marsh above the Yar Bridge, with its Toll House, and Norton Gasworks beyond, are well covered in snow. The nearest ketch is identifiable as the 1864 built *Effort*, 25 reg. tons and Fareham owned. The scene dates from around 1910.

85. ST CARRIER and LSWR tow-boat →

The 1904 Dutch built steam tug *Carrier* has but one lightly laden charge, for this 1908 trip, as she aims across the ebbing tide for the Lymington River. A few barrels and packing cases make up the scant cargo. This 98 grt tug lasted well into Southern Railway days. She was exceptionally beamy for her 60 ft. length, and could carry passengers if required. Later, a smaller steam tug named *Jumsey* operated this service, although tow-boats still occasionally went behind the paddle steamers.

86. JOLLY coasters

Having discharged her coal cargo at Norton Gasworks, this steam coaster is cautiously approaching the 1863 built wooden bridge over the River Yar, en route to the sea. One of a large number of similar sized steamers (400 tons), all with 'Jolly' names, such as *Jolly Laura*, *Jolly Marie* etc, she was owned by Walford Lines of London. They actively traded coastwise in the 1920s and 1930s. Yarmouth Quay's domestic coal trade ceased about 1907. The present Yar Bridge, of the steel, swinging variety, came into service in 1987.

87. Yarmouth, tow-boats galore →

Yachting's popularity was definitely on the increase by the time of this 1930s photograph. Astern of the steam tug, whose capstan is just visible, lay three more 'modern' tow-boats, laden with private cars and their occupants. At this stage these craft had steel hulls, and were of the order of 20 tons apiece. Cars and people had already endured a lengthy embarkation process at Lymington Slipway and now, await the opposite at Yarmouth. Soon, they hope, those stern doors will be lowered and the freedom of uncluttered roads awaits. Each boat could manage several cars of the day, and no doubt prayers were offered up, for absence of rain on voyage - the cars alone affording the only elemental shelter. The first purpose built motor ferry on this route appeared in 1938 - phew! This was the *MV Lymington*, 275 grt and she would serve on this crossing until 1973, later working on the River Clyde for Western Ferries.

88. DEPV FARRINGFORD →

To augment the valiant efforts of the 1938 built Lymington, and cope with post war traffic growth, the unique *Farringford* appeared in 1948. In truth she was a 'paddler' but diesel electric powered. At 489 grt she offered more much needed accommodation for passengers and space for thirty two cars. Serving the Lymington route until 1974, this ferry later operated across the River Humber at Hull, replacing paddle steamers, there.

89. MV FRESHWATER

Taking the name of her 1927 predecessor, in 1959 this 363 grt motor ferry entered service. The photograph, taken at Yarmouth in 1971, shows the ship at the slipway, where such technology as 'linkspans' had yet to appear. *Freshwater* served until 1973.

90. MV BOURNEMOUTH QUEEN →

With the passengers enjoying an exploration of Yarmouth, this 1935 built, 227 grt excursion vessel had come South in 1968 from Scarborough, where she ran as *Coronia*. At the time of this 1971 photograph Croson, Ltd. of Poole, were operating her from Dorset to the West Wight. *Bournemouth Queen* revived the name of a well known Red Funnel paddle steamer of 1908. By the 1980s, the 1935 ship had become a static restaurant at Rochester, on the Medway.

91. MV CARRIER →

Proving just what a popular name this has been down the years, the passing subject of this 2003 scene is a 1993 built, Cypriot flag motor coaster of 2,514 grt. She is of the 'high-hatchway', mini-bulker type, quite common today, and is seen outbound in ballast heading for the Needles Channel, about to overtake a Lymington hopper barge.

92. PS WAVERLEY

Needing little introduction and looking as resplendent as ever, the 1947 built paddle steamer is seen here in 2003, having just called at Yarmouth Pier. Some passengers have disembarked for a couple of hours ashore, and will rejoin later for the run back to Dorset. Yarmouth's splendid 1876 pier, rather like *Waverley* has been cherished and maintained in no small way, by charitable donation, and voluntary endeavour. It has survived and prospered unlike too many of its contemporaries around the coast, and hopefully, long may it continue, so to do.

93. MV CENWULF →

Three of the four 'C' class car ferries built for Island services between 1969 and 1973, now form the Lymington to Yarmouth fleet. These ships have to contend with foot passengers ex Lymington Pier Station, as well as the ever increasing vehicular traffic of today. *Caedmon* and *Cuthred* initially worked on the Portsmouth route, but later the former joined sister ships *Cenwulf* and *Cenred* on the Western Solent. These ships are all of about 760 grt and can carry 750 passengers and 52 cars, although this figure later increased with the addition of portable upper car decks. Over the years, several different liveries have been carried, but the application of adverts more generally on ships, is a recent phenomena. The nature of the Yarmouth to Lymington crossing means the ships spend as much time negotiating the winding Lymington River, as they do at sea. This restriction has so far precluded the introduction of any larger craft, but it cannot be too many years before some form of replacement has to materialise for these three faithful old workhorses.

94. MV BALMORAL →

The 1949 Thorneycroft built, 688 grt *Balmoral* once served Red Funnel's Southampton to West Cowes route. Sold on in 1968, she then ran for Campbell's in the Bristol Channel area, along with *Westward Ho!*, her old running mate, *Vecta* from 1938. By chance, and the sad loss of the *Prince Ivanhoe* (ex.*Shanklin*), the *Balmoral* proved most suitable, to assist in fund raising for the *Waverley* project. The ex Red Funnel ship was put through a major upgrade in 1986 to better suit her for this new role. One major alteration was the elimination of the small after car deck, this area being made into extended accommodation with galley and dining saloon. Strangely, this has improved the ship's profile. Now operating under the Paddle Steamer Preservation Society banner, the ship has subsequently seen much work around many parts of the UK coast. The current light upperworks livery over a dark hull, with light funnel certainly suits her form. Note the planks of Yarmouth's Pier each have a stencilled individual person, or company name - this 'sponsor-a -plank' funding has secured the Pier's integrity, and in this June 2004 photograph both ship and pier look equally smart.

Map No.8 Poole Harbour

(1) Poole Quay
(2) Old Power Station site
(3) Lower Hamworthy - site of today's commercial and cross Channel ferry port.
(4) Sandbanks - Studland chain ferry.

95. C&F NURSE →

Beyond the gaff mizzen sail of the coasting barge *Triton* of London, lies the elegant steel hulled schooner *C&F Nurse*, 98 reg. tons, and built at Falmouth in 1900. Double topsail rigged, she is typical of the many craft coming to Poole Quay to load, often local china clay. Through the schooner's rigging can be seen the open bridge and tall funnel of a steam coaster. Coal for the Bournemouth Gas and Waterworks Company's Pitwines works nearby, came to this quay for many years. The photograph dates from 1917.

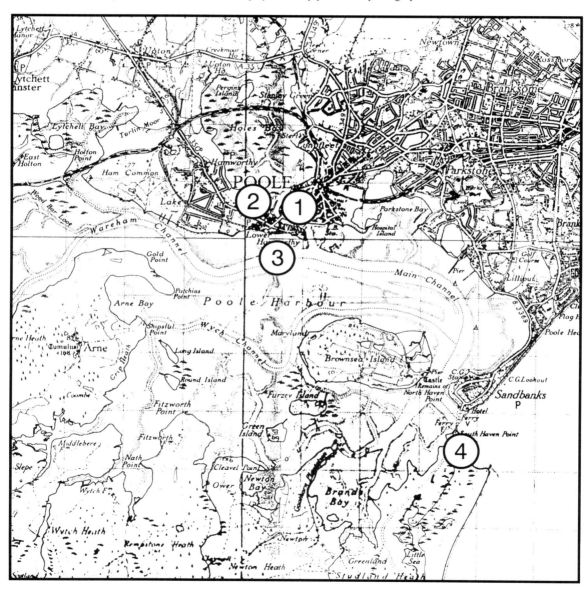

96. MARY WATERS and PS MONARCH (1)

The reverse view at Poole Quay in the 1920's, the schooner this time nearest to the camera is the *Mary Waters* of Jersey, 89 nrt she had been built at Padstow in 1875. On the opposite Hamworthy side a three masted schooner lies against the hulk, whilst Cosens twin funnelled paddler *Monarch* of 1888, awaits business. This old timer served in both World Wars, not being scrapped until 1950. Unusually, for a paddler, she had a proper raised forecastle head and passengers were allowed thereupon.

↙ 97. SS GLENG and MT WENDY ANN

With the local tug *Wendy Ann* at the bow, a big load of sawn Baltic timber is just arriving courtesy of the Norweigian steamer *Gleng*, 1,331 grt 2,050 dwt and built in 1920. Many veteran Scandinavian steamers worked this trade right into the 1960s until modern motor ships finally left them unable to compete. The timber cargo in this early 1950s scene would have been in the order of 500 standards of hand stowed lengths. A couple of decades later, and it would have been brought in metricated packages, drastically reducing the man power required for loading and discharging. The *Wendy Ann* was one of a number of tugs over the years to carry this name. She was run by Harry Rose Towage, who carried out much local work at Poole.

98. RESULT

One of the most familiar sights around the UK coasts for seventy years was the steel hulled schooner *Result*, 125 grt she came from Carrickfergus Shipyard in Northern Ireland, in 1893. In this 1950s Poole photograph she still sports a full schooner rig, although auxiliary motor power had long been installed. Gradually, over the decades her rig was cut down, and engine size increased to help her compete. This she managed to do until finally retiring from trade in 1967, by which time she ran as a fully powered motor ship. Today, *Result* is preserved 'land-based' at the Ulster Folk and Transport Museum, in Northern Ireland.

99. SS POOLE QUAY

Around the time of nationalisation of the electricity industry in 1948, numerous colliers were ordered to serve Southern power stations, with coal supplies. In the case of Poole, the power station site could only be reached by way of the town's lifting bridge, and the Little Channel. A series of six 'Poole' colliers of 1,366 grt 1,700 dwt were constructed at yards in Sunderland, entering service from 1949. Four more identical vessels, *Bodmin Moor, Brent Knoll, Mendip* and *Polden* followed to serve West Country installations. In this 1950s photograph and looking quite new, *Poole Quay* is carrying the BEA (British Electricity Authority) funnel marking. In a sudden policy change, Poole power station went over to oil firing in 1959/60, and when only just over ten years in service, the fleet was sold 'en-bloc' to Associated Portland Cement, for their coastal trades. *Poole Quay* became *Snowcrete*, this lasted but three years more, and she finally went out to Mediterranean owners, ultimately being wrecked in the Gulf of Aqaba in 1978.

100. MV CRANBORNE →

By the 1950s, John Carter (Poole) Ltd. had a small fleet of motor coasters running in the general trades. These ships were all in the 300 to 500 ton range. In 1958 a brand new ship was ordered from the Hoogezand Shipyard in Holland, and duly entered service as *Cranborne*, 439 grt. Seen here in new condition with an unusual but very light load, she has ten or so, caravans on the hatchtops. The only minor inconvenience - where to stow the derricks? Sadly, the fleet survived only a few more years, like many others, in difficult trading conditions.

101. MV SAND SNIPE ↘

J.Bolson and Company, Shipbuilders at Poole started in 1922 and by the 1950s were building various types of coastal ships. This example, one of several similar owned by South Coast Shipping of Southampton, entered service in 1961. *Sand Snipe* 517grt became familiar along the south coast, delivering sea dredged aggregates for the building industry. Seen here in laden condition, with the suction dredging pipe secured, and the last excess hold water draining from the scuppers, she is about to enter port. The additional foremast lamp arrays give the night time signal for a dredger at work.

102. Poole Quay and MV PURBECK PRIDE

By the millennium end, Poole Quay itself had been forsaken by cargo carrying vessels. Such remaining trade, (coal had long since departed) either moved across to the Hamworthy side, or had been integrated into the roll-on, roll-off system, also on that side of the harbour. In this 1999 scene, the carriage of tourists in and around Poole's huge natural harbour has taken over. A variety of craft, including *Purbeck Pride*, on the Brownsea Island run, are here joined by one of the Army's landing craft.

103. MV OCEAN DEFENDER →

Moored adjacent to the futuristic art sculpture on the Quay in 1999 is the ecological charity Earthkind's ship *Ocean Defender,* a converted trawler open to the public, to highlight their cause.

104. Poole's commercial port of Hamworthy ↘

Almost loaded beneath Bulwark Quay's large Scotch-derrick type crane, is the Portuguese cargo vessel *Dombate*, unusually registered in the Island of Madeira. Nearer the camera in this 1999 scene are the Harbour Commissioners' grab dredger *C.H.Horn*, 159 grt of 1958, and the hopper barge *Hop* 209 grt of 1955; vital craft for the maintenance of any active commercial port.

105. Old and new industries

This scene along the Hamworthy side reflects a mix of conventional shipping and the growing importance of leisure industry technology. Exclusively styled motor cruisers constructed here by Sunseekers, are just part of this general trend, securing many jobs in the marine sector.

106. MT HERBERT BALLAM →

To assist the larger ships using Poole Harbour now in 1998, the motor tug *Herbert Ballam*, 95 grt entered service. This 1,300 BHP diesel tug was the last ship to be built at the old Bolson Yard, and is seen here at her regular mooring just across from her berth place, looking very smart in the Commissioners' fleet livery.

107. Poole Lifting Bridge →

The only direct road link from the Town to the Hamworthy side is via Poole's venerable lifting bridge, which still has to be opened for masted vessels to pass, to and from Holes Bay, beyond. Plans are now afoot for a second structure to ease congestion, and the workload of the old bridge. The timber wharf can be seen just to the right in this 1999 photograph.

108. Fishermen and working craft.

Beyond the inshore fishing boats, an interesting assortment of workaday craft lie moored above the bridge. The nearest tug is the 1960 built *Carron Highlander*, 192 grt and once named *Erimus Cross*. The second smaller tug is the 76 grt *Kingston Lacy* also from 1960, and once Shoreham's harbour tug where she ran as *Kingston Buci*—a local name in those parts. Further to the right is an ex Admiralty fleet tender and finally, just visible, one end of a previous Sandbanks chain ferry in this 1999 scene.

109. MV TORCH →

Once a standard motor cargo coaster type from 1964, after various owners and name changes this ship was converted in 1977 for the role of buoy tender. She operated on the River Clyde, replacing an elderly steamer of the same name. Apart from the installation of a crane to access the after end of the hold, the ship's profile is little altered from cargo days. In 1999 *Torch* is seen moored in Holes Bay.

110. MB HOP →

Seen earlier as a non-propelled barge, the 1955 built craft has been converted to a fully powered motor hopper. With the addition of what amounts to a 'bolt-on' power package right aft, and provision of a modern wheelhouse, radar and signal mast, *Hop* has become a most useful vessel, no longer tug dependent, and with the ability to work much further afield.

111. MVs PURBECK PRINCESS and SOLENT SCENE

Several neatly kept excursion craft line the Quay in 2004, awaiting the crowds for harbour trips to Brownsea
Island, Sandbanks, etc. Although the last excursion paddle steamers have been gone for almost four decades,
there seems to be quite a healthy revival in the small ship excursion trade, throughout the Solent region,
affording much seasonal employment for crews and operators. *Solent Scene*, 131 grt was built at Bideford,
and dates from 1974.

112. MV POOLE BELLE and Sandbanks Chain Ferry

The seagoing excursion vessel is seen here outbound in showery August 2004 weather. She regularly visits a number of places from Swanage to Yarmouth in the summer tourist season. Meanwhile, having awaited a clear channel, the Swanage to Sandbanks chain ferry trundles back to the Poole side, on her short constrained passage.

113.   BRAMBLE
BUSH BAY

A deck full of motor cars are poised to run ashore at Sandbanks, having saved many motoring miles on the Swanage to Poole trip, avoiding the circuitous route around Poole Harbour's extensive upper reaches, via Wareham.

114. MV CONDOR VITESSE ↗

Bearing absolutely no resemblance to the earlier sail, steam and motor vessels that have graced Poole Harbour, Condor Ferries' high speed catamaran type *Condor Vitesse* is seen entering the port in 2004. The 1997 built 5,005 grt 'wave-piercing', Incat type craft belongs to a group of similar vessels operating on many routes around the World. They are certainly fast with speeds up to 39 knots, but are susceptible to reliability problems when faced with higher sea and swell states, when compared to the more traditional hull forms.

115.   MV BARFLEUR →

Measuring just over 20,000 grt a few years back craft of this size were unheard of on any cross - Channel route. Indeed, until 1970 few such vessels exceeded 5,000 grt *Barfleur* dates from 1992, and now handles much of the car and freight traffic on the Poole to Cherbourg run. She is seen here in 2004 outward bound passing Sandbanks.

116. PS CONSUL

Three of the area's last excursion paddle steamers will be fondly remembered by many today. These old stalwarts belonged to the firm of Cosens Ltd. of Weymouth, Dorset. Although from a little further west than the main study area of this book, the ships of this 1852 founded company were such frequent visitors in the summer tourist trade to the Solent, as to warrant inclusion. The company's operations ceased in 1966. Built in 1896, the 277 grt *Consul* came to the area in 1938 from Devon where she had worked as *Duke of Devonshire*. Her small size enabled excursion landings to such venues as Lulworth Cove, where 'over-the- bow' access to the beach was the only way. In 1962/3 she briefly ran along the Sussex Coast, after sale by Cosens. The photograph at Weymouth dates from the 1950s.

117. PS MONARCH (2) ↗

Reviving the name of the popular twin funnelled ship from 1888, this one was 1924 built at Southampton as *Shanklin* (1) for the Southern Railway. The 399 grt ship ran between Portsmouth and Ryde until the new motor vessel of the same name appeared in 1951, thence she moved west to join the Weymouth fleet, renaming as *Monarch*. In the photograph she looks little different to her Solent ferry days, and has a good number of passengers onboard. The scrapyard awaited in 1962.

118. PS EMBASSY →

Proving just how popular old railway steamers were, the 1911 built *Embassy* had also plied the Portsmouth to Ryde route, as *Duchess of Norfolk*. From 1937 to 1967 when Continental breakers claimed her, Cosens employed her in the Weymouth, Swanage, Bournemouth and Isle of Wight areas; the very last survivor of their fleet.

Map No.9 Cowes / River Medina / Newport / Wootton Creek

(1) West Cowes, linked by chain ferry to -
(2) East Cowes
(3) Medina Railway Wharf
(4) Island Harbour Marina
(5) Cement Mills Wharf
(6) Newport Quay
(7) Wootton Bridge / Old Mill
(8) Fishbourne car ferry terminal.

119. ARROW →

Built at Cowes in 1875, the 20 reg.ton gaff rigged ketch *Arrow* represents a group of craft that were loosely termed the 'Cowes ketches'. Generally in the 20-40 ton range, they traded to all the minor and major ports in the area from Chichester to Poole. The photograph dates from the 1930s and this particular vessel owned by Shepard Brothers, Ltd. of Newport held the distinction of being the last one of her type to trade under sail alone (1938). The legendary *Bee* of 1801 sailed in the Solent trades for a recorded one hundred and twenty five years.

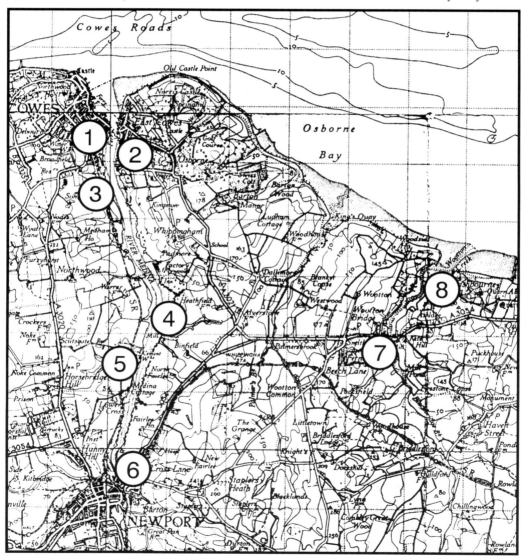

120. MB OCEANIC

Captured here inbound at Cowes in her later motorised trading days around 1960, is the barge *Oceanic*. Built in Holland in 1903, she once formed part of Thames owner Goldsmiths' huge fleet of coastal sailing barges. 158 grt and steel hulled, her spritsail barge rig was cut down in 1941 and a motor installed. In the photograph, the old mainmast stump serves principally to carry the masthead 'steaming' light. The hatch boards are stacked fore and aft of the hatchway ready to work cargo and the addition of a curiously shed-like wheelhouse did little to enhance her appearance. Her usefulness unquestionable, she survived, working for Vectis Shipping until the 1970s - no mean career. Any comparison between this old time barge and the new '*Blade Runner*' types of 2003, is impossible to draw.

121. MB WESSEX

Originally one of the larger wooden coastal sailing ketches, the 1918 Littlehampton built, 148 grt *Wessex* could carry well over two hundred tons of cargo. A decade or so into service, auxiliary engines were fitted and reliance on the wind in the ketch rig ended. By the 1930s she traded for Charles Price of Newport. Sister barge *Moultonian* of 1919 (the last built at Littlehampton) ran for Thomas Price, and later Vectis Shipping. *Wessex* ended her career trading for Williams Shipping of Southampton in 1955. In the 1950s photograph the barge is running simply as a motor vessel, with the lower part of her mast utilised for derrick work. The small wheelhouse would not have been an original provision.

122. MTB BLADE RUNNER ONE

This is an entirely new type of barge locally, and specially designed as her name suggests for the carriage of wind turbine blades. The 2000 built craft is of the 'deck barge' type, there being no traditional hold, also extra shallow in draught to access the Company's Newport berth on the River Medina, where the factory is sited. Good manoeuvring capability is another necessity. In this 2001 photograph she is arriving from Southampton for more blades. This kind of specialist operation by water is vital as such cargo movement by road would be nigh on impossible; an all too rare success story for water transportation in an era dominated by road freight.

123. SS GURNARD

Pilots have been taken out by boat to be placed aboard homecoming merchantmen for centuries, their local knowledge and expertise being of paramount importance in guiding ships into harbour. Steam pilot cutters later became stationed strategically off many of the country's main port approaches. Often cutters remained on station for a week at a time, outgoing pilots then stayed aboard, until it was their rota turn to pick up an incoming ship, thus returning home. In this 1950s photograph the Cammell, Laird, Birkenhead built 342 grt *Gurnard*, of 1932 was one such ship. The transfer launch swung outboard in its davits is ready for action. Note the cooling water outlet has a cover directing water downwards - and not down the boatman's or pilot's neck! The construction of this sturdy little ship, with the upper deck continuing straight out of the forecastle head, was such to enable maintenance of the pilot station in all weathers. In the last few decades, the remaining motor pilot cutters have given way to a shore based high speed launch service. No longer do pilots have to endure cramped, pitching quarters out 'on station', awaiting that inbound ship.

124. MV SUSAN CONSTANT

J.Samuel White & Companys' Cowes Shipyard opened
for business in 1803, and rapidly gained a reputation
for the construction of fine, well found and seaworthy
craft. Sailing warships for the Navy, and commercial
craft of many types came off the slipways, for the next
one hundred and sixty years. Soon, steam packets,
cargo and passenger paddle steamers, craft for overseas
river use, ferries, motor coasters, lightships, lifeboats
and modern naval warfare vessels, were launched into
the River Medina. The output was quite prodigious,
but in common with most other UK yards, overseas
competition grew just too fierce. The Company ceased
building ships in 1965, and three examples of the final
years of production are next described, all significant
merchant vessels, ending such activity at Cowes.
At 352ft.loa the cargo ship *Susan Constant* 3,464grt
4,850dwt represents the larger end of ship construction
achieved at Cowes. By 1958 Constants Ltd were
replacing steamers with motor ships of more modern
economical design. In this photograph from when the
ship was new, a full cargo of pit props, including deck
load is required to bring the ship down to her marks.
The derricks are lashed to the masts out of the way, and
interestingly even in 1958, radar was still not being fitted
to some new merchantmen.

125. SS SARNIA →

One of an identical pair, the other being *Caesarea*,
steam turbine propulsion for cross - Channel ferries
was nearing its end in 1960. This 3,989 grt vessel had
been ordered by the British Transport Commission
(BR), to operate the Weymouth to Channel Islands run.
The 1965 photograph shows the ship in subsequent
British Rail blue hull and red funnel livery - that two-
way track arrow logo just did not look quite right on
many of the fleet's ships.

126. MV CRESCENCE →

A very old firm indeed, mentioned variously within this
book, the London and Rochester Trading Company
had begun life with a fleet of sailing barges. Their
houseflag trade mark of a crescent moon, and reddish
brown hulls, were most distinctive. In short, they soon
became known as Crescent Shipping. As the sailing
barge era dwindled, the Company turned to motor
barges and coasters in a big way. When in 1965 the 999
grt *Crescence* entered the waters of the Medina, she
was her owner's largest. With patent folding, tracked
hatch covers, the ship would carry coal or any dry bulk
commodity, shore loaded and discharged. Masts with
derricks were disappearing at this time. This ship was
radar fitted from new.

127. MV NORRIS CASTLE

Following in the wake of a converted landing craft (the first *Norris Castle*), the 1958 version emerged from Thorneycrofts' Shipyard, purpose built to give greater car and lorry capacity on the Southampton to Cowes run. The 734 grt ship would later be much modified, with additional passenger accommodation, giving a rather different profile to that seen here in 1971. In 1994, she went out to the Adriatic Sea for further service.

128. MV NETLEY CASTLE

Red Funnel's first true 'double-ender' entered service in 1974. Representing a further size increase to 1,183 grt she could carry more of the ever growing freight trucks, or 87 cars. Unusually, this ship had a bridge 'conning' position at both ends of the superstructure block. *Netley Castle* sailed on until the introduction of the 'Raptor' class ships in 1994. She too, found further work out in the Adriatic area. Photograph 1980s.

129. MV WIGHTSTONE

The second ship in the Solent area to carry the name, this 1967 built motor coaster of 438 grt was under no less than her 8th name here in 2001 entering Cowes Harbour. She had started out as the Belgian coaster *Andre*, but thirty years later found employment as a sand carrier around the Solent. The earlier ship of the same name was the ex steam collier *Brent Knoll*, converted in the early 1960s to a motor driven sand suction dredger.

130. MT BARDSEY →

The crescent moon emblem has been up-graded on the altered funnel markings of the coastal tanker *Bardsey* 1,144 grt of 1981. This ship and sister vessel *Barmouth* have spent most of their careers working around the UK coast, despite their Japanese origin, which was not common at the time. The scene dates from 2003.

131. MV RYSUM →

Here seen outward bound in ballast from Medina Wharf in 2004, is the 1992 built, 2,450 dwt coaster *Rysum*. With a retractable wheelhouse and lowerable masts, etc. she belongs to a type now popular in the European coastal trades known as LAD's. This stands for low air draught, equally at home on sea passages, or the great inland waterway systems of Europe. These ships are now frequent visitors to many British ports.

132. MT WILCHALLENGE

Small tugs are another group of vessels whose appearance has changed radically in recent years. Motor exhausts often no longer emanate from traditional funnels. Looking very smart indeed in Williams Shipping of Southampton livery, she is seen here entering the Medina in 2003. This vessel is just one of a range of sizes of tug built in Holland today.

133. MV HOO VENTURE

One of the last major flag operators of small dry cargo ships in the UK today, is the Lapthorn Company of Hoo, Kent. They have specialised in what became known as standard coaster designs from the Yorkshire Drydock Company of Hull. *Hoo Venture* at 498 grt from 1982 is a twin screw single hatch vessel of the smaller class, so built. She has been retro-fitted with a hydraulic excavator type 'cargo shifter', a very successful application of shore based technology. These items are proving very effective and efficient in the coastal trades today, and are a far cry from the ponderous workings of traditional derricks and winches. The need for shore craneage is also eliminated. The ship is seen entering Cowes in 2002.

↖ 134. MV RED JET IV

In 1969 Red Funnel introduced a high speed passenger only service between Southampton and West Cowes, initially using the 'Shearwater' class of hydrofoil ferries. By 1991 passenger number increases saw the introduction of the first 'Red Jet' catamaran type on the route. *Red Jet IV*, a still larger variant entered service in 2003, and in the photograph is gently edging out of the Cowes fairway. Once clear, she will accelerate up to thirty knots plus, for the trip to Southampton.

← 135. MV RED EAGLE

With that ever growing car, truck and coach traffic across the Solent, Red Funnel introduced their next generation of vehicular / passenger ferries from 1994. Named after raptors, *Red Eagle* 3,028 grt has slight design differences from the first two ships, including a higher bridge structure. Yet further car capacity would be added ten years later, by a clever 'jumboisation' project in Poland, which would see the installation of a fixed upper, full length car deck to these ships.

136. MB TARWAY

Craft of this size had been familiar in trades to the River Medina for a century or more, but most had gone by the 1970s. In this 2003 photograph the little motor barge *Tarway* 80 grt 140 dwt and dating from 1955, is seen arriving with a load of stone. Unusually, for such a tiny ship she could also engage in dredging work, hence the long pipe and gear visible on deck.

137. ALBATROS

Something very rare indeed, a ship that has actually sailed during three centuries - *Albatros* , 128 grt began life in 1899 as a Dutch sailing cargo ship. She is steel hulled and ketch rigged, and in this 2002 photograph would look little different from 1899. Built at Capelle, she would originally have traded around the Baltic, North Sea and UK coasts, later running as a motor ship in Denmark, before being beautifully restored and returned to trade, for a second cargo carrying career. As recently as 1991 *Albatros* lifted grain from Newport Quay to the Mainland. Now finally retired from trade, she is still actively sailed, and on occasion visits Cowes Week.

138. THV MERMAID

With a large navigation buoy on her foredeck beneath the high capacity derrick, *Mermaid* is seen anchored off Cowes in 2001, where her Trinity House operators have maintained a base for decades. Korean built in 1987, this 2,820 grt ship, along with sister vessels, maintain the myriad of buoys and lights all around the English and Welsh Coasts. The open, clear after deck permits the operation of a small helicopter, to maintain the remoter, unmanned automatic light structures.

← 139. MV FASTCAT RYDE

Not normally present in Red Funnel territory, Wightlink's 1985 built, 478 grt fast ferry is arriving at Cowes during the special Cowes Week 2003 service from Lymington. Ryde Pier to Portsmouth Harbour Station, is the normal sphere of operation.

← 140. MTB BLADE RUNNER TWO

Greatly reflecting the success of her smaller sister barge, this vessel has the bridge / conning position right forward in the bow. The extremely long, clear after deck is capable of transporting lengthier wind turbine blades to the Mainland. In this 2004 photograph she has just left the Island behind, en route to Southampton with several blades on deck.

141. MTB BLADE RUNNER ONE at East Cowes

Wind turbine blades wait on the Quayside for shipment in 2004, in front of the well known giant Union Flag at East Cowes. The emblem has graced the massive doors of this building since the Queen's silver jubilee year of 1977. Saunders Roe, British Hovercraft and British Aerospace have all variously used the giant hangar, over the years.

← 142. West Cowes waterfront

On a summer's day, a continuous stream of yachts and motor cruisers of all shapes and sizes pass in and out of the River Medina, to and from the many upstream marinas. In this 2002 photograph, the 1911 erected hammer head crane at Samuel White and Company's old premises stands high, beyond the cross river chain ferry. Now a rare national survivor, originally it was rated at 80 tons lifting capacity, and although much down rated in lifting ability, it has remained in use throughout. The little Cowes owned tug *Hofland*, lies between the barge and the chain ferry.

← 143. MV RED FALCON

Compare this 2004 photograph to that of the sister vessel (no.135), and the extent of enlargement to include the new full length upper car deck is very apparent. This has, of course, necessitated similar shore based modifications, to enable shipboard access. The total car capacity is now 200.

144. MT BREAKSEA

Arriving with supplies is the 1985 built 992 grt motor tanker *Breaksea*, another unit of the Crescent fleet. For examples of their craft in much earlier times - see nos 126, 155 and 159.

145. SSs ABANA, NELL JESS, ELLINGTON and T.G.HUTTON

Quite why no less than four venerable coasting steamers lay abreast at Medina Wharf c1900 is unknown, however the scene makes for a fascinating delve into coastal shipping over a century ago. So many shipping companies have come and gone, some had but one ship, others entire fleets. We examine each ship in turn.

SS ABANA

Built in 1871 this 729 grt vessel came from James Laing's Sunderland Yard, and formed part of a large fleet owned by James Westoll. She went to Greek owners in 1906. The nearest ship to Medina Wharf, she has the very old fashioned wooden rails around the poop deck, also sails brailed into the masts. The latter still applies to three of the four steamers here.

SS NELL JESS

Positively the youngster of the quartet and the only 'engines aft' type present, *Nell Jess* dates from 1896 and came from S.Macnight's, Ayr, shipyard. She was of 496 grt and owned by the Goole and West Riding S.S. Company. This ship survived until the 1950s, trading out in Brazil.

SS T.G.HUTTON

At 703 grt this 1893 built steamer also came from a Sunderland yard, that of Short Brothers, and she traded for Henry Cochrane, from that port. Note, navigation bridges were still mostly of the open variety - the only weather protection being a canvas wind and spray 'dodger'. Chart rooms were always one deck below with open bridges.

SS ELLINGTON

Outboard of all is, amazingly, another steamer of identical tonnage, the *Ellington* of Newcastle, operated by Freear ↗

↙ and Dix, not too far from her birthplace of D.Baxter's Shipyard at Sunderland, in 1891. In all probability the ships had brought coal for the Island, the rail tracks and trucks on Medina Wharf just being visible in the photograph. The Cowes and Newport Railway Company opened this wooden pier type wharf in 1877, with the aim of attracting bulk coal cargoes for onward rail distribution around the Island. Not until Southern Railway days would improvements be made in the form of the present solid straight quay arrangement (1928). Coal transporter cranes were also duly added. The wisdom of the early railway company was well found, for up to 150,000 tons of coal were needed per annum until the 1960s.

146. SS CAMBERWAY

Another ship managed by Freear and Dix, this 1919 built, 782 grt steam coaster with midship's bridge was owned by the Sunderland Steam Ship Company. Some incremental design changes can be seen compared to the earlier steamers. A proper closed-in wheelhouse has been provided and the age old provision of sails, has not. However, in this 1920s photograph the wharf has yet to be altered from its 1877 profile.

147. MV BALTISKIY-110

Eighty years later, the 2004 view across the Medina to the wharf of the same name shows great changes. The railway tracks, coal transporters and paraphernalia of coal importing days have vanished - removed in 1974. Now general dry bulk commodities are handled, and in this instance grain is being poured into the holds of a 1980 built Russian freighter of 1,926 grt 2,554 dwt. She is just one unit of a large class of ships, and clearly shows the growing size of tonnage reaching this facility nowadays.

148. NORA-AV-VEN →

Moving upstream, on the east bank of the Medina at Binfield a marina has been developed complete with access lock, in recent decades. In this 1985 photograph, the ex Swedish coastal sailing ketch *Nora-Av-Ven* has found a new calling in the form of a 'Pirate Feasts' restaurant. She has been re-rigged as a double topsail schooner, and later moved up river to Newport Quay, opening to the public as 'The Pirate Ship'.

149. PS MEDWAY QUEEN →

Seen here looking very smart in 1971 eight years after retirement, the 1924 built Dunkirk veteran shared this location for some years with *Ryde*, (last season 1969). *Medway Queen*, 316 grt became by far the luckier of the two, after subsequent years of dereliction, in 1984 she was returned by barge to the Medway, where gradual restoration proceeds, care of the Medway Queen Preservation Society.

150. PS RYDE (afloat)

Denny of Dumbarton built the 566 grt ferry in 1937 for the Southern Railway's Portsmouth to Ryde service, as a sister ship to the 1934 *Sandown* - (scrapped in 1960s). *Ryde* later became known as *Ryde Queen* , opening as a night club once she had been permanently grounded in her own specially constructed 'lagoon'. Beyond, in this 1971 scene, the sand dredger *Baymead*, 340 grt and once the coastal tanker *Chartsman*, is proceeding upriver to Newport.

151. PS RYDE (last resting place) →

Still looking at least cosmetically reasonable in 1993, in truth the old paddler was in steep decline structurally, and would become a sad rusting, holed, tidal wreck with little prospect of betterment.

152. MT BATSMAN →

In 1985 the small tanker *Batsman* is just arriving at the old Cement Mills Wharf, upriver on the opposite bank to no.151 This 1962 built, 217 grt ship is specially designed for shallow river / under bridges type work, on the Thames for example. Owners, Bowker and King ran a sizeable fleet of coastal, and river tankers in the 1960s and 70s. The wharves here once witnessed the production of 'home grown' cement, manufactured from local, rail delivered chalk from a quarry near Newport. The plant closed before World War II, after which a reception facility for the product was opened, to receive coaster cargoes from the Mainland.

← 153. MVs ASH LAKE and FORMALITY

Two interesting little motor coasters lay at the wharf in 1971. Nearest is the locally owned, blue hulled, *Ash Lake*, 198 grt dating from 1939. She was previously the Dutch coaster *Dina*. This ship brought bagged cement to the Island in the traditional way. The black hulled vessel astern is F.T.Everard's *Formality* of 1968, 200 grt and yet of a design that could carry 400 tons of bulk cement. The specially designed cement unloader system can be seen working the ship's hold. This ship belonged to a series called XL400's - several owners ran them and yet within a few years they too were outsized and outmoded, in the ever quickening search for economy of scale in sea transportation.

← 154. Newport, the River Medina

This early down river photograph from around 1900 shows new piling to the right of the silty channel, at low tide. The quay extension was much needed to ease congestion at the town's existing wharves, as even at this time craft, and their numbers were growing in size rapidly. Sitting bolt upright in the main channel is a big trading ketch, whilst at the new, but as yet barren quayside, a couple of smaller local versions, lie moored. Today the space on the east bank houses - the Bus Museum, Classic Boat Museum and a hotel and restaurant, where all manner of cargo passed for over a century, or so. This same change of circumstance has been seen at the majority of places visited. The west bank delights in the name of Little London.

155. CABBY

Moored at the warehouse berth of Crouchers Ltd; is the 1928 built spritsail barge *Cabby*, 76 tons. She had the honour of ending wooden hulled sailing barge construction on the River Medway, and traded for the London and Rochester Co. In this 1930s study, she is working a sacked cargo at the tightly 'pinched' berth between the old Sandown railway line arches, and the warehouses. *Cabby* remained in trade until the 1960s, the warehouse site is now a car park. Judging by many of the seemingly impossible tight corners that sailing barges used to reach, it is scarcely surprising that commentators used to say they 'could float on wet grass'. One factor to please the crew on this visit - they did not have to lower all sailing gear to pass beyond Newport's rail bridge.

156. Newport Railway Bridge and HESTER

The old commercial heart of Newport Quay, literally at the 'foot' of the town, became sliced in two with the advent of the railways. Between 1862 and 1875, no less than four separate companies had lines radiating out, spoke-like, from the Island's capital. Right from the start, frequent opening of the rail bridge was required, when the tide had risen sufficiently, to enable tall masted craft

to pass. This, of course, could disrupt the Victorian sense of well ordered timetables. In the pre 1900 scene, local ketches and cutters crowd the quays, each side of the retractable spans. The signalman, leaning out of the box window, is doubtless wondering when next to summon the opening gang - the tide is high! By the 1960s, barge visits above the bridge were rare, as craft grew larger and berthed downstream. At the end of 1966, trains no longer passed overhead, as the Ryde to Cowes line closed. On the left in the photograph is the 18 reg.ton *Ellen* of Cowes, built in 1869 and owned by Thomas Arnell of Newport. On the Little London side, lies the 1872, Emsworth built, Portsmouth registered, *Hester* a ketch of 17 tons. Two good examples of the tiniest cargo carriers of their day.

157. MB MFH

British Road Services appeared in 1948 under the Government Nationalisation plans. Earlier firms such as Crouchers, Shepards, Carter Paterson and Pickfords had all been involved with cross-Solent cargo traffic. The *MFH* of Cowes, a typical mid 20th century motor barge, was one of the last to percolate upstream of

the bridge in 1962. In the photograph, the gang of 'winders' are peering down on the interruption, as she gently nudges through. This uncommon photograph clearly shows the two separate spans withdrawn to the west side. There were always two separate running lines over the bridge - the Sandown line nearest the camera, whist the further span supported the Ryde line. The Sandown span was taken away some years before closure of the Ryde to Cowes line.

158.   Newport's new road bridge and
         NORA-AV-VEN

When this scene was photographed in 1988, the old railway bridge and infrastructure had been demolished, to be replaced almost at the same spot by a dual carriageway road supporting bridge. St Thomas Church tower, in the background continues to preside having seen it all—the coming, and the going of both ships; and railways. The 'Pirate Ship' as *Nora-Av-Ven* became known, has shifted upriver, and acquired a white hull. Yachts replace barges and warehouses make desirable residences, when so converted.

159.   IRONSIDES

Spritsail barges have been a familiar sight on the Medina for about one hundred and fifty years. Their ability to be handled by one man and his mate, made them very economical to work. Some later and larger units were built at Southampton, and had steel hulls. *Ironsides* belonged to the steel hulled category, although built at Grays, Essex in 1900, the 78 reg. ton barge was yet another London and Rochester Company vessel. By the 1950s, many surviving barges lost their lofty rigs in deference to motorisation, among the last such craft to convert, anywhere. A good many then continued to work as motor barges, in their old sailing haunts. Today, a number of these lovely old craft have been fully restored to actively sail again, and may be seen at corporate events, or regattas and of course, Cowes Week. This 2001 scene tells all - a barge and a quay, both retired from active trade.

160. Odessa Shipyard

The splendidly named Odessa Shipyard at Little London Quay, Newport surely ranks as one of the most picturesque, seen here in 1929. One freshly white painted craft is up on the slipway for attention, seemingly stern first, and just a handful of small boats line the placid tide line.

161. Odessa Shipyard in 1969 and MB FIELD →

Some forty years after photo no.160, British Road Services motor barge *Field* is up on the slipway receiving underwater attention. Built in 1949, the 133 grt vessel did not have many more years to trade across the Solent. Barge traffic was in steep decline by the 1960s, in deference to road haulage. This time, the cottage sports a new coat of white paint, yet the aspect beyond is still 'rural'.

162. Royal Naval Steam Picket Boat →

Seen attending a 'steam boat' rally at Newport Quay in 2004, is a beautifully restored steam launch from the Royal Naval Museum in Portsmouth. The smartly turned out crew are equally as immaculate as the brass topped, bell-mouthed funnel, glinting in the sunshine. Modern industrial units however, now form the backdrop.

163. Barges at Newport Quay

The scene is1951, with five typical 'Newport' barges sitting on the mud, awaiting the incoming tide, four of which may be identified:-

CROP : 33 grt 1950 built British Road Services motor barge.

CHAMOIS : this 1917 built, wooden hulled, 44 grt vessel had previously run for Crouchers.

FOX : built at Plymouth in 1898, of 26 grt she too, had run for Crouchers in earlier years, and also had a wooden hull.

MASK : another British Road Services motor barge. 'Hunt' names such as MFI (Master of Foxhounds), had long been a traditional naming feature of Island barges. The Carter Paterson advert on the Stores wall proclaims the daily Mainland service, for those so interested in shifting their wares. Over the nearest barge on the right can be seen one of the distinctive quayside hand cranes, with its battered metal umbrella. A similar operable crane exists to this day, further along the quay.

164. SS LECONFIELD →

Launched in 1936 at Dartmouth, the 91 grt steam grab dredger started life working at Littlehampton Harbour, keeping the River Arun's channels in check. She came to work in the Solent area in the 1960s, and by the time of this 1973 photograph was awaiting just one thing - the scrap man. In earlier years the ship carried a steam powered, dredging grab crane.

165. MB CELTIC

Just retired from the bagged cement trade in 1969 is the Dutch built, 153 grt 1903 built motor barge *Celtic*. Steel hulled, and originally fully rigged as a spritsail sailing barge, she was one of a quartet surviving many years in trade. (see also-*Oceanic*). In 1941 motors were fitted and after World War II, Captain Alf Sheaf brought the old ship to Newport. Subsequently, she spent the next twenty odd years bringing in the Island's cement in bagged form from Asham Cement works, on the River Ouse between Newhaven and Lewes, in Sussex. A typical load was about 230 tons and after closure of that works, Shoreham or the Thames were the origination points. By 1969, the ex Dutch coaster *Ash Lake* (described elsewhere) had taken over. By the year 2000 the old *Celtic* had been partly restored to sailing rig, at a North Kent barge museum.

166. MV VECTIS ISLE

In 1969, Vectis Shipping bought the 1939 built, 213 grt Dutch coaster *Badzo*. Dutch owners were 'up-sizing' their fleet at this time, and a number of these useful little vessels came to the British flag. Shallow draught and good carrying capacity for their size, went hand in hand with such places as the Medina. The ship traded later for the fledgeling Carisbrooke Shipping Company, finally passing to Panamanian owners as *Estrella IV*. This 1971 photograph at Newport, shows her looking very smart, and in common with many, in deference to the trends of the day, she has lost that single, central mast and two derricks, so distinctive of this type, when built. Shore craneage now predominated for cargo work. Subsequently, Carisbrooke Shipping has grown from strength to strength, gradually building up a large fleet of modern cargo ships up to 19,000 tons capacity, for World-wide trading - most definitely unable to enter their Company's birthplace - the River Medina.

167. MV ANJA

Another ex Dutchman photographed at Newport Quay in 1971, this 1940 built ship of 262 grt has acquired a bright red livery, and also lost her original cargo gear. A simple pole mast now supports the masthead navigation light. Craft of this type were among the largest to reach so far into the River Medina.

168. MV ASH LAKE (in retirement)

The successor to the barge *Celtic* is seen here in 1991, also out of trade. She remained moored at Newport Quay for several years. Unlike the other Dutch 'schoots' as they were termed, this one retained that mast and derrick arrangement until the end. *Ash Lake* had traded as *Dina* before coming to the British flag, she was of 198 grt and dated from 1939.

169. MB NEEDLES

Moored along the quay in 1969 are two of the final barge types in the British Road Services fleet. Nearest is the 1960 built, 93 grt *Needles*. In another decade, 'day-boats' to the Mainland would pass into history, as road haulage won the battle, in conjunction with the larger ferries. Interestingly, *Needles* later found rather different employment in the west of Ireland - servicing a fish farm.

170. MV COLBY RIVER

One of Newport's greatest natural drawbacks as a port has always been that shallow depth of water, traffic being subject to tidely restricted bursts of navigation. In this 1991 scene, the sand carrier *Colby River* is awaiting sufficient water for departure. Built in 1969, she was another member of the standard XL400 type of small motor coaster, and had entered service as *Tower Marie* for Tower Shipping. Shortly after this photograph was taken, she acquired the local name *Medina River*. Beyond can be seen *Ash Lake* and *Nora-Av-Ven*.

171. MB CALBOURNE

At high tide the river north of Newport looks quite wide and important. This is the scene in that direction from the site of the previous shot, looking towards Cowes, and the Solent. That is where this 103 grt 1952 built barge was launched from Whites' yard, for their Island Transport Company. With her curiously off-centre funnel she has remained locally and been converted to a houseboat. *Medina River* went foreign for further trading in 1998.

172. *ex.* MFV YELLOWFIN

Trawlers, by virtue of their occupation, were a rare sight at Newport. The wooden hulled, 115 grt, 1945 built *Yellowfin* had started her fishing career as *Alorburn* , with the Lowestoft registration number of LT282, despite construction at Looe, in Cornwall. Later she operated from the Cornish fishing port of Newlyn, but was long out of the fishing business by the time of the 1973 photograph. A small crane can be seen on deck, and before too much longer she was stripped of all fixtures and fittings, and decommissioned. Her propeller remains set on a plinth at the Sea Street entrance to Newport Quay, today.

173. MB TARWAY and MV ARILD

The last regularly used wharf, Blackhouse Quay at Newport is seen here in 2003 from across the river, with two local traders alongside. *Tarway*, already described, and the ex Scandinavian *Arild*, 199 grt have both recently been engaged in the aggregates trade from the Mainland.

174. MTB BLADE RUNNER ONE (loading) →

In the 2003 scene, barge *ONE* is at the specially constructed berth adjacent to the factory. This consists of two 'finger' piers, between which the craft lays. A large straddle carrier then runs out astride the barge's deck to lower the blades onboard. The bow of the barge is directly below the point where the two blades meet. Already one is onboard, resting beneath the vessel's elevated wheelhouse. The whole carefully orchestrated operation, must of necessity occur during suitable 'tidal windows'.

175. EDITH at Wootton Bridge Mill →

A few miles east of the Medina lies Wootton Creek. The pre 1900 wintry scene shows the Portsmouth built ketch *Edith*, 42 reg.tons and dating from 1875, she was owned by J.T.Crampton. She has a boom and gin block rigged ready for cargo handling, at the mill. The building dated from the late 1700s and survived until 1962, no trace remains today. Note the old mill stones leaning against the wall, and another small trading vessel's bow peering around the corner.

176. Fishbourne car ferry first slipway.

With a narrow concrete slipway, and some simple piling to guide the ferry in, this basic 1927 arrangement would suffice hereabouts, for over thirty years. The little ferries, *Wootton*, *Hilsea* and *Fishbourne* had to, also. Angled at ninety degrees to Wootton Creek, sixteen cars would not take long to load or unload. However, these basic facilities represented a quantum leap from the 'tow-boats' preceding. Your author's shorts appear to be anything but, in this 1957 scene!

177. MV FISHBOURNE (2) → second Slipway.

In 1961, by slewing the entire operation through ninety degrees to align with the creek, the second generation of car ferries could better be accommodated at Fishbourne. The 293 grt ship of the same name is starting to disembark her 34 cars, or whatever, including a caravan. The pier for the ships to moor against is seen here in 1966 to the left of the ferry. Swans and cygnets seem little perturbed by the activity nearby.

178. Onboard- Easter 1967 →

There were not many cars on this trip - Pickford's low-loader traversed the Solent many times in 1967 bringing 'new', old electric trains to work the Island's shortened remaining line from Ryde Pier to Shanklin. Island railway stock has invariably been formed of someone else's left-offs throughout its history, this was no exception, since these carriages had already put in thirty years service on the London Underground. The stock was built between 1925 and 1934. This photograph makes an interesting comparison to a 1913 stock transfer - see no.191.

179. MV CUTHRED

The lead vessel of the third generation of Fishbourne ferries had just entered service here in 1969. This vessel sported a full width passenger saloon on high, over the car deck, could carry fifty two cars, and measured in at 704 grt. Although road freight vehicles were expanding, they had not yet reached the 'juggernaut' proportions familiar everywhere, today. This is the period when 'door to door' carriage of goods, and the roll-on, roll-off system system expanded most rapidly, causing the virtual cessation of traditional barge traffic, locally.

180. Fishbourne's third terminal

Wightlink's *St.Catherine* has just arrived from Gun Wharf, Portsmouth, and is gently edging up to the linkspan at what has become the third version of Fishbourne terminal. Now, the creekside berth sees the ferries moored port side to the pier, at what has become a twenty four hour operation, excepting Christmas day. The scene dates from 2004.

Map No.10 Ryde to Bembridge

(1)   Ryde Esplanade
(2)   Spring Vale Beach
(3)   St. Helens Quay
(4)   Bembridge

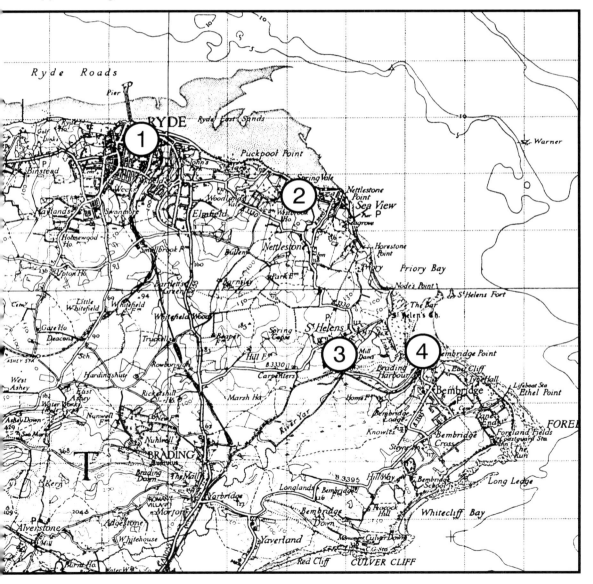

181. The Port of Ryde in the 19th Century

An apt description, judging by the activity caught here on camera in the late 1800s. With the railway pier distant, a diverse group of local traders may be seen in the little dock. Cut into the harbour wall, it was situated adjacent to George Street slipway. Just visible over the wall is the 17 ton *Dove* of 1824. On the further wall a couple of rail trucks are sited some distance from any rail lines. One ketch marked clearly with 'Transit Ryde' is either drying her sails, or setting out on voyage. The railway wagons were hauled by horse along the 1864 tramway between Pier Head and St. Johns Road station. This was replaced by a railway line under the Esplanade in 1880.

182. MB JJC

The age old practice of beaching ships to load or unload by horse and cart, had evidently not quite died out here on Ryde Sands, in the 1920s. Patient cart horses either side of the barge, have firm sand for just a few hours to support

hooves and cartwheels. The location for this photograph was probably about half way between the gaff sail and the pier in No.181. *JJC*, 36 grt was a small, steel hulled motor barge built at Amsterdam in 1910. By 1923 she was running across the Solent for J.J.C.Stevens, of Portsmouth, and would have carried 50-60 tons of coal, or whatever. Enough to keep a number of small carts, horses and carters, dashing to and fro, whilst the tide was out.

183. ASTEROID at Ryde

Chaplin and Company's 'boomie' ketch of 1884, and 24 reg.tons is rigged typically for cargo handling the old way, boom and gin-tackle. This waterfront location was particularly exposed to northerly blows, and of course, totally tide dependent. Pre 1927, the steam tugs had delivered 'tow-boats' to Ryde's George Street slipway, now squeezed out of

existence between the Esplanade Railway Station, and the Hovercraft Terminal, of today. On the quayside may be seen various goods in transit and a couple of horse drawn vans. Note the profile of buildings across the road.

184. The Hovercraft Slipway

The buildings just referred to in no.183 oversee the popular Hovercraft service to Southsea Beach, started in 1965 and now operated using 100 seater craft by Hovertravel. Truly 'light years' from the wooden cargo sailing vessels, steam tugs and 'tow-boats' of old, one short length of stone quayside does still exist, along by the Esplanade Station, complete with the iron mooring bollards. This lies behind the airborne hovercraft seen here in 2004.

185. PS SHANKLIN

The image of a paddler turning away from Ryde Pier Head towards Portsmouth is one that will be familiar to many, although usually decks were 'awash' with trippers. In this 1928 photograph, *Shanklin* is seen in her original Southern Railway, open bridge form. Thorneycrofts of Southampton built her in 1924 (see no.117 for later career), and she was one of the last to have open side alleyways each side of the after saloon. Most paddle steamers without wheelhouses had certainly acquired one by the end of World War II. *Shanklin*, together with sister vessel *Merstone*, did not go off on Naval minesweeping duties as so many of her contemporaries had done, but maintained the Island link.

186. Ryde Pier Head

Whilst much of the seaward end of Ryde Pier now daily resembles a commuters car park, the continuing existence, in such good order, of a pair of Chateris, 1925 electric cranes is amazing. Their main occupation until the traditional ferries departed, was the loading and unloading of mail skips, and whatever might have been in the ferry's small hold. Similar cranes survive at the Portsmouth Harbour Station end, as well.

187. Ryde's Victoria Pier

Largely forgotten today, this pier came and went during the Railway Pier's long life. Built in 1859, it ran out from a short distance east of its grander neighbour, for something like half the length. It was reportedly none too successful a venture, and by 1922, had succumbed to demolition. Beyond the Pier some ocean sailing ships can just be discerned, with the usual local smaller craft inshore, about to sit on the mud.

188. Spring Vale Beach

This scene around 1900 just east of Ryde shows a spritsail barge deftly put ashore, exactly parallel to the sea wall, and as close as possible. Careful observation of the detail reveals just what is happening. Between the little girl in the white dress standing alone on the beach, and a stack of timber close to the barge, can be seen a specially constructed raised 'trackway'. Made out of something like 12" by 12" baulks of timber, it is the guideway for the departure of a massive, obsolete cannon by the girl's side, with gun barrel end-on, to the camera. It is likely that such items were being shipped away from the nearby Puckpool Battery. No doubt a day or two's calm weather had been hoped for - the barge is in the half-tide position, and very securely moored. A vast army of labourers would be required to move and load the old gun aboard. Such manual skills have all but vanished today, in our hydraulic crane era.

189. ALFRED at St.Helens Mill

Tide mills were a popular and early form of mechanisation, long before steam power made its debut. As the tide peaked, sluices would be shut to capture a damned headwater, upstream of the mill. As the tide receded, the miller would control the outflow of water, thus harnessing its power via the mill wheel, to turn the corn grinding mill stones. The large mill at St. Helens dated from about 1780 and would have seen one hundred years service before the coming of the railways, locally. Detail in this 1880s photograph is quite astonishing. To the left of the building, workers are shifting sacks using a cart and pair of horses. From the *Alfred's* boom and block, a whip rope is gravity loading flour sacks to be lowered into the hold, direct from a first floor doorway. Another cart and pair waits with what appears to be a load of straw, while over to the right, the coalman's cart is laden and ready for the rounds. Amidst this hive of local industry, it is possible to find about fourteen workers in total. And some are aware of a new phenomena - posing for the camera! This particular mill carried out considerable seaborne trade. *Alfred* dated from 1835, measured 19 reg tons and was built at Southampton. By 1900 she was trading for Edward Way, of Newport.

190. SS ALLERWASH →

By the 1880s, Bembridge Harbour had quite serious siltation problems, as already touched upon herein. In 1896 a major dredging exercise took place to deepen and straighten the navigable channels. In this splendid 1900s scene with the Downs beyond, the veteran steam collier *Allerwash*, 381 grt and dating from 1861, has brought coal to St. Helens Quay. This old timer had been lengthened in 1876, and ran for decades in the North East to South Coast coal trade, often to the Solent area. She traded on into the 1920s, and certainly still carried sails when photographed. *Allerwash* was particularly identifiable by her incredibly tall funnel, plus the 'schooner-like', three masted rig. (the mizzen mast is behind the tree). The mill building described in no.189 was just off to the left in this picture, whilst the smart Victorian style house is still there today.

191. St.Helens Quay: railway arrivals

Thirty years had passed since *PS Carrier's* brief struggle with the rail truck service to this spot from Langstone. Evidently, and probably with not just a little difficulty, seaborne railway stock could still come ashore here in 1913. A large gang of workers, baulks of timber and lengths of rail, have been made into a disembarkation track for five coaches, plus steam engine, from the barge. Second hand railway vehicles have come ashore at various locations during the Island's railway history - even at this point items were becoming heavier - the barge had to be big enough for about eighty tons of stock yet suitable to navigate Bembridge Harbour, by tug.

192. Barge, Loco No.734 and carriages.

No doubt elated by safely landing the first nine ton coach, the team pose for the camera, and steel themselves for the bigger challenge of shifting a twenty eight ton tank engine. High tide and daylight most probably concentrated minds. At this point, a digression from shipping to railway history perhaps may be forgiven, for No.734 has had the honour of making two grand entrances on the Island, and of course so far, only one departure, in its 128 year career to date.

1876	A1 class No.46 'Newington' built at Brighton for the LB&SC Railway Co.
1903	Sold to the L&SW Railway Co; to work the Lyme Regis branch.
1913	Hired by the Freshwater, Yarmouth and Newport Railway.
1914	Bought outright by the FYNR and it became No.2 'Freshwater'
1938	Re-numbered W8 by the Southern Railway.
1949	Returned to the Mainland by British Railways re-numbered 32646
1963	Withdrawn on closure of the Hayling Island branch.
1966	Sold to Brewers Brickwoods - placed outside the Hayling Billy Pub.
1979	Donated to the Wight Locomotive Society, and in June that year returned on a low-loader via the Fishbourne car ferry.
2004	Running on the Island Steam Railway as W8 'Freshwater'.

193. St. Helens Quay in 2004 ↗

This corner of Bembridge Harbour once lay on the shores of the far larger Brading Haven. For centuries, trading ships could reach a quay quite close to the ancient town of Brading. That age-old problem of silting continued apace, and eventually attempts were made to reclaim the harbour from the sea. By the mid to late 1800s, Brading Quay became inaccessible by ship, and with the 1882 opening of the Brading to Bembridge branch line, the remaining area above St. Helens gradually became arable land. A large modern stone built house now stands where the mill dominated. The shallow arch bridge in the *Alfred* scene, is still there today, along with the Victorian house, now painted cream. The quays to the left now support modern dwellings where rail sidings and industry flourished. Yachts replace colliers.

194. PS ISLAND QUEEN

A very grand hotel was constructed in Bembridge to welcome visitors off the newly arrived railway line. In fact the Royal Spithead Hotel opened some time before the first train arrived in 1882. The hotel also attracted visitors by way of its own small pier nearby. From the late Victorian period until World War One, several small paddle steamers operated locally to Seaview Pier and across to Southsea. One or two of these vessels were locally owned. In the photograph from the 1890s, and with steam from her safety valve obliterating the funnel top, the 97 grt *Island Queen* is manned ready for action, awaiting passengers. She dated from 1878, but by 1900 went out to the Gibraltar area for further service. The pier remained unused after the War, not being demolished until 1928.

← 195. SL FERRY KING

Little altered from Portsmouth to Gosport ferry days, the 57 grt 1918 Camper and Nicholson built steamer, is seen here at rest in Bembridge Harbour in the 1960s. Shortly, she would be converted to diesel propulsion, to re-enter service locally as *Solent Queen*, in the excursion business.

← 196. MB SIRIUS

Lying in much the same location some forty years later is the mooring / salvage barge *Sirius*. Her old fashioned, bluff hull form belies River Humber origins.

197. The Nab Tower's birthplace

All mariners rounding the eastern tip of the Isle of Wight, and most locals are familiar with the form of the Nab Tower and light structure, a few miles south east of Bembridge. Until 1920, a lightship had warned shipping entering the Solent of the dangers at the Nab shoal. During World War One, three large 'mystery' towers were constructed just inside the entrance to Shoreham Harbour, in Sussex. Greatly shrouded in secrecy at the time, their ultimate intended use was thought to have been as submarine net / defensive structures, across the Dover Strait. However, when the war ended in 1918, only one tower had been completed, so the Admiralty duly towed it out to sea in 1920, on a one way journey to the Nab. The Nab Light Tower was born, and continues as a navigation mark and light to this day, warning all Portsmouth and Southampton bound shipping. It is easy to see from this photograph how craft navigating too close could readily gash their hulls, as only the dark iron-work part protrudes above the waves. The remaining tower, and a bit, were ignominiously dismantled at Shoreham, by 1924.

198. MV VILLE and Ventnor Haven construction →

In the 1860s, the Ventnor Pier and Harbour Company planned to make a harbour between two piers at the increasingly popular health resort. Mother nature seemed unamused and decided otherwise, wrecking efforts in short order. In 1887, a pier of the iron piling variety, opened to afford Victorians their expected pleasures of promenading and steamer trips. This structure survived for one hundred years before it too, was claimed by the elements. The year 2003 saw work begin on a small but attractive boat haven, as part of Southern Water's major local upgrade project. Now Ventnor again has a focal point along its Esplanade. Technology today being more advanced in construction terms, has seen new breakwaters robustly built, and the method employed certainly merits examination. The 499 grt Finnish vessel *Ville*, built in 1985, loads enormous granite stone blocks from the 'mother ship' *Anja C.*, anchored a mile or two beyond. That ship is fitted with a powerful hydraulic claw fitted crane, to lower the rocks onto the smaller ship's four side-tipping, deck hoppers, as the two lie moored together. When sufficient rise of tide permits, *Ville* came inshore to the appropriate spot to tip the rocks just where required, as can be seen in the photograph. Already, the haven outline is emerging, and one can only hope the driver of the excavator had a lifejacket and could swim.

Map No.11 Ventnor to St. Catherines Point

(1)   Ventnor Boat Haven.   (2)   St. Catherines Tower.   (3)   St. Catherines Lighthouse

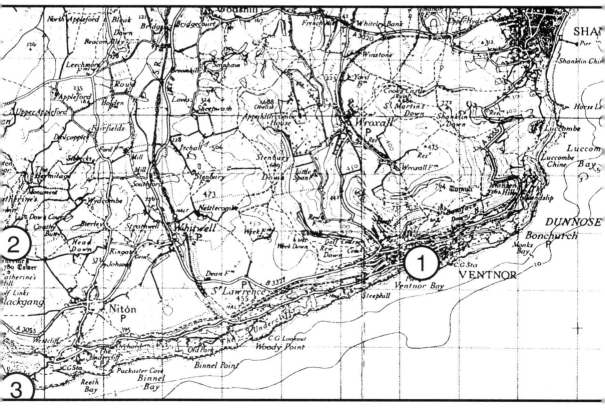

199. The completed Haven

Topped by a new bandstand, seen here in 2004, the fruits of the *Ville's* labour can be admired in the sunshine. A few boats have taken up their moorings, already.

200. St. Catherines Tower

The high land mass at the Island's most southerly point affords a suitable spot to end these local voyageings. This lofty location has been a major landfall sighting for ships bound up Channel, for as long as there have been ships. The stone tower in the 2004 photograph has witnessed all for centuries, from its elevated spot. Otherwise known as the Chantry or Oratory, at 800 ft above sea level it has served as a navigation aid, since the 1300s, if somewhat erratically. The stretch of coastline beyond is littered with rock ledges, extending some distance off-shore, from the time when the land itself did just that. One especially dangerous 'prong' of rocks extends out from Atherfield Point, just visible as a line of disturbed water, in the photograph. Very many scores of fine sailing ships, and later a number of steamers were wrecked on this ledge, lost in fog or storm, or simply by the unwary.

In 1314, one such vessel, the St. Mary, laden with 174 tuns of wine, came to grief along this section of coast, her crew, mercifully, were saved. A local landowner declared he had the right to salved cargo. Walter de Godeton had picked the wrong

cargo owners to test his theory. The wine belonged to a Monastery in Acquitane, and the Church would most certainly not allow the matter to rest. Walter, was required to have constructed a warning light to shipping. Choosing existing monastic buildings on top of St. Catherines Down, the tower became a lighthouse, and thenceforth a Monk was assigned to keep the light (fire), burning. This state of affairs worked for centuries, until Henry VIII saw fit to cause the dissolution of the Monasteries- mariners beware - no light for several more centuries!

In 1780, the forefathers of Trinity House built another structure nearby, however it suffered from the same basic shortcoming as its predecessor, it simply could not be seen from sea level whenever there was mist, fog or low cloud. Finally, in 1838 the modern low-level site at St. Catherines Point was sensibly chosen, highly visible to mariners, as indeed it is to this day. The delightful old octagonal stone tower, is now well maintained, serving both as a distinctive land and seamark, and memorial to one Walter de Godeton. Close inspection of the stonework just over the two lower openings, reveals the V-shaped outline cut, where the oratory roof once abutted. At 800 ft. elevation, the sea horizon is about thirty three miles away, and since the tower also stands no less than one and a quarter miles back from the shoreline, it is scarcely surprising that such a gallant venture was none too successful.

The area beyond, betwixt sea and downs is locally known as the 'Back of the Wight'. We have now arrived at the back of the book.

Bibliography

Back of the Wight	1934	Fred. Mew	-
A History of the Southern Railway	1936	C.F.Dendy Marshall	-
The Ports of the United Kingdom	1939	Sir David J.Owen	-
London's Lost Route to the Sea	1965	P.A.L.Vine	-
South Eastern Sail	1972	Michael Bouquet	0 715355 92 9
Sailorman between the Wars	1978	John Allendale	-
The Ancient Town of Yarmouth	1981	C.W.R.Winter	0 9501779 7 0
Gas and Electricity Colliers	1984	D.Ridley Chesterton R.S.Fenton	0 905617 33 9
Sealink Isle of Wight	1989	John Hendy	0 9513093 3 1
The Steam Collier Fleets	1990	J.A.Macrea C.V.Waine	0 905184 12 2
Whites of Cowes	1993	David L.Williams	1 85794 011 3
Red Funnel	1997	Michael Archbold	-
Commodore Shipping	1997	Kevin Le Scelleur	0 9531466 0 X
Ferry Services of the L.B.& S.C.R.	1998	S.Jordan	0 85361 52 17

Lloyds Registers
Mercantile Navy Lists
World Ship Society-Marine News
Shipping Magazines
Local Newspapers

INDEX

ABANA	145	C&F NURSE	95
ABERCRAIG	54	C.H.HORN	104
ALBATROS	137	CABBY	155
Albert Johnson Quay	28	CAEDMON	93
ALFRED	189	CAESAREA	125
ALLERWASH	190	CALBOURNE	171
ALLORBURN	172	Camber Dock	30
ANDRE	129	CAMBERWAY	146
ANJA	167	CAROLA	77
ANJA C	198	CARRIER PS	13/191
ARCO SEVERN	57	CARRIER ST	85
ARILD	173	CARRIER MV	91
ARROW	119	CARRON HIGHLANDER	108
ASH LAKE	153/168	CELTIC	165
ASHLEIGH-R	56	CENRED	93
ASTEROID	183	CENWULF	93
ATTENDANT	62	CHAMOIS	163
ATTUNITY	54	CHARTSMAN	150
BADZO	166	Chichester Ship Canal	1
BALMORAL	94	COLBY RIVER	170
BALTISKIY-110	147	CONDOR VITESSE	114
BARDSEY	130	CONSUL	116
BARMOUTH	130	Continental Ferry Port	43
BARFLEUR	115	CORONIA	90
BAT	45	Cosens,Ltd	116
BATSMAN	152	Cowes Chain Ferry	142
BAYMEAD	150	Cowes Waterfront	142
Beaulieu River	74	CRANBORNE	100
BEE	119	CRESCENCE	126
Bembridge Harbour	194	CROP	163
BESSIE	70	CUTHRED	93/179
BLACK PEARL	16	CYMBA	10
BLADE RUNNER ONE	122/174	DEAL	63
BLADE RUNNER TWO	140	Dell Quay	6
BODMIN MOOR	99	DOMBATE	104
BOISTERENCE	69	DONALD REDFORD	51
BOISTEROUS	69	DOVE	181
Bosham Quay	7	DUCHESS OF FIFE	22
BOURNEMOUTH QUEEN	90	DUCHESS OF NORFOLK	118
BRADING	24	DUKE OF DEVONSHIRE	116
BRAMBLE BUSH BAY	113	DUKE OF YORK	76
BREAKSEA	144	EBBRIX	29
BRENT KNOLL	129	ECHO	11
BRISTOLIAN	42	EDITH	175
Broad Street Slipway 1.	25	EFFORT	84
Broad Street Slipway 2.	33	EGREMONT	3
Bucklers Hard	74/75	EL MANSOOR SAAIL	35

Eling Creek	72	HUMBER STAR	66
Eling Wharves	71	Hythe Ferry	57
Eling Tide Mill	73	IRONSIDES	159
ELLEN	156	ISLAND QUEEN	194
ELLINGTON	145	ISLE OF GUERNSEY	61
EMBASSY	118	ISLE OF JERSEY	61
EMPIRE FARRIER	64	ISLE OF SARK	61
Emsworth Harbour	9	Itchen, ferry punts	49
EOLUS	16	Itchen, floating bridge	50
ERIMUS CROSS	108	Itchen, River	52
ERNIE SPEARING	54	JAYNEE W	37
ESTRELLA IV	166	JJC	182
Fareham Quay	44	JOLLY 'coasters'	86
Fareham Ballast Quay	46	JUMSEY	85
Fareham Flour Mill	45	JUPITER	3
FARRINGFORD	88	KINGSTON BUCI	108
FASTCAT RYDE	139	KINGSTON LACY	108
FERRY KING	195	Langstone Wharves	15
FERRY QUEEN	31	LECONFIELD	164
FIELD	161	LORD ELGIN (pass)	59
FISHBOURNE 1.	25	LORD ELGIN (cargo)	60
FISHBOURNE 2.	177	LOYAL WATCHER	41
Fishbourne Terminals	176/7/80	LYMINGTON	87
FLATHOUSE	28	Lymington Pier	79
Flathouse Quay	28/43	Lymington River	78
FORMALITY	153	Lymington, Town Quay	82
Foster,J.D.,Emsworth	9	Little London	154
FOX	163	MARINE VENTURE	40
FRESHWATER PS	55/81	MARY WATERS	96
FRESHWATER MV	89	MASK	163
GLENG	97	MEDINA RIVER	170
Gosport Chain Ferry	21	Medina Wharf	145/6/7
Gosport Slipway	19	MEDWAY QUEEN	149
GREAT EXPECTATIONS	57	MENDIP	99
Gun Wharf	32	MERMAID	138
GURNARD	123	MERSTONE	185
HAMEN	27	MFH	157
Hamworthy	104	MONARCH PS 1.	96
Hayling Ferry	17/18	MONARCH PS 2.	117
Hayling Rail Bridge	15	MOULTONIAN	121
HENRIETTE B	30	MYRTLE	80
HERBERT BALLAM	106	Mystery Tower	197
HESTER	156	Nab Tower	197
HILSEA	25	NEEDLES	169
HOFLAND	142	NELL JESS	145
HOO VENTURE	133	NETLEY CASTLE	128
HOP	104/110	Newport Rail Bridge	156
HOTSPUR IV	57	Newport Road Bridge	158
Hovercraft Terminal	184	Newport Quay	163
HUELIN DESPATCH	37	NORA-AV-VEN	148/158

NORRIS CASTLE	127	SHANKLIN MV	24/34
Northam Bridge	47	SHANKLIN PS	117/185
Norton Gasworks	86	SHEARWATER	134
OCEAN DEFENDER	103	SHIELDHALL	65
OCEANIC	120	SIRIUS	196
Ocean Village	56	SKELLIG ROCK	68
Odessa Shipyard	160/1	SLATEFORD	80
ORSELINA	29	SNOWCRETE	99
OUR LADY PAMELA	37	SOLENT PS	78
OUR LADY PATRICIA	37	SOLENT QUEEN	195
PILOT	83	SOLENT SCENE	111
'Pirate Ship'	148/158	SOUTHAMPTON PS	58
Pitwines	95	SOUTHAMPTON BELLE	20
Point Wharf	34	Southgate Basin	3
POLDEN	99	SOUTHSEA	24/48
POMPEY LIGHT	26	Spring Vale Beach	188
POMPEY POWER	26	STADT ESSEN	30
POOLE BELLE	112	ST.CATHERINE	36
Poole Lifting Bridge	107	St.Catherines Tower	200
POOLE QUAY	99	ST.CLARE	38/39
Poole Quay	102	ST.EILIAN	58
Port of Ryde	181	ST.HELEN	40
PRINCE	19	St.Helens Quay	191/193
PRINCE IVANHOE	24	St.Helens Mill	189
PURBECK PRIDE	102	Steam engine No.734	192
PURBECK PRINCESS	111	SUSAN CONSTANT	124
RECOIL	10	SUSSEX QUEEN	55
RED EAGLE	135	SWANAGE QUEEN	55
RED FALCON	143	SWIFTSURE	76
RED JET IV	134	TARWAY	136
RESULT	98	T.G.HUTTON	145
River Medina	154	TORCH	109
ROSIE	47	'Tow-boats'	85/87
ROUSTEL	68	TOWER MARIE	170
ROYAL FIRTH	80	TRITON	95
ROYALIST	34	VADNE	23
Royal Naval Steam Picket	162	VECTA	94
Royal Pier, Southampton	58	VECTIS ISLE	166
Royal Spithead Hotel	194	Ventnor Haven	198/9
RYDE	150/1	VERE	4
Ryde Railway Pier	186	Vernon,HMS (base)	32
Ryde Victoria Pier	187	VESTA II	20
RYSUM	131	VICTORY, HMS	19
Salterns Lock	4	VILLE	198
Salterns Jetty	16	VITA	31
SANDOWN	24/150	Vosper Thorneycroft Yard	53
SAND DIVER	64	WADE STONE	66
SAND SNIPE	101	WARRIOR, HMS	37
Sandbanks Ferry	112	WAVERLEY PS	92
SARNIA	125	WENDY ANN	97

WESSEX	121	Wootton Bridge Mill	175
WESTWARD HO!	94	Wootton Creek	175
White, Samuel J. & Co.	124	XXXX	82
WHIPPINGHAM	24	Yar, River	86
WHITCHALLENGER	67	Yarmouth Harbour	83
WHITSPRAY	42	Yarmouth Pier	92
WIGHTSTONE	129	Yarmouth Quay	84
WILCHALLENGE	132	YELLOWFIN	172
WOOTTON	25		

Acknowledgements

I would like to record thanks and appreciation to all the kind individuals, Societies and Organisations, who with their time, information and material, have so helped in the compilation of this book. In particular: Harold Appleyard, A.R.Carder, Geoff Cotton, Tessa Daines, Barbara Deacon, Peter Frankland, Susan Hill, Bob Irwin, Dr. John Mackett, Steve Marshall, Peter Mumford, Phil Neumann, Terry Nigh, Wayne Pritchett, Roger Silsbury, David Taylor, David Watkins, and Colin West.

Photographic Sources:
Beken of Cowes 119, Bembridge Heritage Society 191,192, Eling & Totton Heritage Centre 70,71, Emsworth Museum 10,11, Hughes.J.A (Photographers,Southsea)   45, Isle of Wight County Record Office 145,189,190,194, Judges Postcards Ltd.Hastings (01424 420919) 95, National Maritime Museum, Greenwich 13, Nigh,W.J. & Sons Ltd. 163, Poole Waterfront Museum 97,98 (Poole Museum Service- Copyright Reserved) Portsmouth Museum and Records Office 25,30, Salmon, J.Ltd; Sevenoaks 82 (Copyright J.Salmon Ltd, Sevenoaks), St. Barbes Museum, Lymington 80, Skyfotos 26,27,28,29,6 0,61,62,63,99, 100,110 123,124, 125,126, Southampton City Council Archive Services 49, West Sussex Record Office 6,7, World Ship Society 54, 64,101,120,

Photographers, where known-

F.N.Broderick,Jnr	189
Rev. Robert Lewes Dashwood	83,84,85
Dr. D.L.Mountford	10
D.Macgregor / D.Rudkin	11
Dr. John Mackett	47
E.W.Mudge	76
R.S.Langley	160,176

The Ordnance Survey maps are from 1930 and are at the scale of 1ins to 1 mile.

MP **Middleton Press**

EVOLVING THE ULTIMATE RAIL ENCYCLOPEDIA

Easebourne Lane, Midhurst, West Sussex.
GU29 9AZ   Tel:01730 813169

www.middletonpress.co.uk   email:info@middletonpress.co.uk
A-0 906520   B-1 873793   C-1 901706   D-1 904474

OOP Out of Print at time of printing - Please check current availability   **BROCHURE AVAILABLE SHOWING NEW TITLES**

A
Abergavenny to Merthyr C 91 5
Aldgate & Stepney Tramways B 70 7
Allhallows - Branch Line to A 62 2
Alton - Branch Lines to A 11 8
Andover to Southampton A 82 7
Ascot - Branch Lines around A 64 9
Ashburton - Branch Line to B 95 2
Ashford - Steam to Eurostar B 67 7
Ashford to Dover A 48 7
Austrian Narrow Gauge D 04 7
Avonmouth - BL around D 42 X
B
Banbury to Birmingham D 27 6
Barking to Southend C 80 X
Barnet & Finchley Tramways B 93 6
Barry - BL around D 50 0
Basingstoke to Salisbury A 89 4
Bath Green Park to Bristol C 36 2
Bath to Evercreech Junction A 60 6
Bath Tramways B 86 3
Battle over Portsmouth 1940 A 29 0
Battle over Sussex 1940 A 79 7
Bedford to Wellingborough D 31 4
Betwixt Petersfield & Midhurst A 94 0
Blitz over Sussex 1941-42 B 35 9
Bodmin - Branch Lines around B 83 9
Bognor at War 1939-45 B 59 6
Bombers over Sussex 1943-45 B 51 0
Bournemouth & Poole Trys B 47 2 OOP
Bournemouth to Evercreech Jn A 46 0
Bournemouth to Weymouth A 57 6
Bournemouth Trolleybuses C 10 9
Bradford Trolleybuses D 19 5
Brecon to Neath D 43 8
Brecon to Newport D 16 0
Brickmaking in Sussex B 19 7
Brightons Tramways B 02 2
Brighton to Eastbourne A 16 9
Brighton to Worthing A 03 7
Bristols Tramways B 57 X
Bristol to Taunton D 03 9
Bromley South to Rochester B 23 5 OOP
Bude - Branch Line to B 29 4
Burnham to Evercreech Jn A 68 1
Burton & Ashby Tramways C 51 6
C
Camberwell & West Norwood Tys B 22 7
Canterbury - Branch Lines around B 58 8
Caterham & Tattenham Corner B 25 1
Changing Midhurst C 15 X
Chard and Yeovil - BLs around C 30 3
Charing Cross to Dartford A 75 4
Charing Cross to Orpington A 96 7
Cheddar - Branch Line to B 90 1
Cheltenham to Andover C 43 5
Chesterfield Tramways D 37 3
Chesterfield Trolleybuses D 51 9
Chichester to Portsmouth A 14 2 OOP
Clapham & Streatham Tramways B 97 9
Clapham Junction - 50 yrs C 06 0
Clapham Junction to Beckenham Jn B 36 7
Clevedon & Portishead - BLs to D 18 7
Collectors Trains, Trolleys & Trams D 29 2
Cornish Narrow Gauge D 56 X
Crawley to Littlehampton A 34 7
Cromer - Branch Lines around C 26 5
Croydons Tramways B 42 1
Croydons Trolleybuses B 73 1 OOP
Croydon to East Grinstead B 48 0
Crystal Palace (HL) & Catford Loop A 87 8
D
Darlington Trolleybuses D 33 0
Dartford to Sittingbourne B 34 0
Derby Tramways D 17 9
Derby Trolleybuses C 72 9
Derwent Valley - Branch Line to the D 06 3
Didcot to Banbury D 02 0
Didcot to Swindon C 84 2
Didcot to Winchester C 13 3
Douglas to Peel C 88 5
Douglas to Port Erin C 55 9
Douglas to Ramsey D 39 X
Dover's Tramways B 24 3
Dover to Ramsgate A 78 9
E
Ealing to Slough C 42 7
Eastbourne to Hastings A 27 4

East Cornwall Mineral Railways D 22 5
East Croydon to Three Bridges A 53 3
East Grinstead - Branch Lines to A 07 X
East Ham & West Ham Tramways B 52 9
East Kent Light Railway A 61 4
East London - Branch Lines of C 44 3
East London Line B 80 4
East Ridings Secret Resistance D 21 7
Edgware & Willesden Tramways C 18 4
Effingham Junction - BLs around A 74 6
Eltham & Woolwich Tramways B 74 X
Ely to Cambridge D 55 1 - PUB APRIL
Ely to Kings Lynn C 53 2
Ely to Norwich C 90 7
Embankment & Waterloo Tramways B 41 3
Enfield & Wood Green Trys C 03 6 OOP
Enfield Town & Palace Gates - BL to D 32 2
Epsom to Horsham A 30 4
Euston to Harrow & Wealdstone C 89 3
Exeter & Taunton Tramways B 32 4
Exeter to Barnstaple B 15 4
Exeter to Newton Abbot C 49 4
Exeter to Tavistock B 69 3
Exmouth - Branch Lines to B 00 6 OOP
F
Fairford - Branch Line to A 52 5
Falmouth, Helston & St. Ives - BL to C 74 5
Fareham to Salisbury A 67 3
Faversham to Dover B 05 7 OOP
Felixstowe & Aldeburgh - BL to D 20 9
Fenchurch Street to Barking C 20 6
Festiniog - 50 yrs of enterprise C 83 4
Festiniog in the Fifties B 68 5
Festiniog in the Sixties B 91 X
Finsbury Park to Alexandra Palace C 02 8
Frome to Bristol B 77 4
Fulwell - Trams, Trolleys & Buses D 11 X
G
Garraway Father & Son A 20 7 OOP
Gloucester to Bristol D 35 7
Gosport & Horndean Trys B 92 8 OOP
Gosport - Branch Lines around A 36 3
Great Yarmouth Tramways D 13 6
Greenwich & Dartford Tramways B 14 6 OOP
Guildford to Redhill A 63 0
H
Hammersmith & Hounslow Trys C 33 8
Hampshire Narrow Gauge D 36 5
Hampshire Waterways A 84 3 OOP
Hampstead & Highgate Tramways B 53 7
Harrow to Watford D 14 4
Hastings to Ashford A 37 1 OOP
Hastings Tramways B 18 9
Hastings Trolleybuses B 81 2 OOP
Hawkhurst - Branch Line to A 66 5
Hayling - Branch Line to A 12 6
Haywards Heath to Seaford A 28 2 OOP
Henley, Windsor & Marlow - BL to C77 X
Hereford to Newport D 54 3
Hitchin to Peterborough D 07 1
Holborn & Finsbury Tramways B 79 0
Holborn Viaduct to Lewisham A 81 9
Horsham - Branch Lines to A 02 9
Huddersfield Trolleybuses C 92 3
Hull Trolleybuses D 24 1
Huntingdon - Branch Lines around A 93 2
I
Ilford & Barking Tramways B 61 8
Ilford to Shenfield C 97 4
Ilfracombe - Branch Line to B 21 9
Ilkeston & Glossop Tramways D 40 3
Industrial Rlys of the South East A 09 6
Ipswich to Saxmundham C 41 9 OOP
Isle of Wight Lines - 50 yrs C 12 5
K
Kent & East Sussex Waterways A 72 X
Kent Narrow Gauge C 45 1
Kingsbridge - Branch Line to C 98 2
Kingston & Hounslow Loops A 83 5
Kingston & Wimbledon Tramways B 56 1
Kingswear - Branch Line to C 17 6
L
Lambourn - Branch Line to C 70 2
Launceston & Princetown - BL to C 19 2
Lewisham & Catford Tramways B 26 X
Lewisham to Dartford A 92 4
Lines around Wimbledon B 75 8
Liverpool Street to Chingford D 01 2

Liverpool Street to Ilford C 34 6
Liverpool Tramways - Eastern C 04 4
Liverpool Tramways - Northern C 46 X
Liverpool Tramways - Southern C 23 0
London Bridge to Addiscombe B 20 0 OOP
London Bridge to East Croydon A 58 4
London Chatham & Dover Railway A 88 6
London Termini - Past and Proposed D 00 4
London to Portsmouth Waterways B 43 X
Longmoor - Branch Lines to A 41 X
Looe - Branch Line to C 22 2
Lyme Regis - Branch Line to A 45 2
Lynton - Branch Line to B 04 9
M
Maidstone & Chatham Tramways B 40 5
Maidstone Trolleybuses C 00 1 OOP
March - Branch Lines around B 09 X
Margate & Ramsgate Tramways C 52 4
Marylebone to Rickmansworth D49 7
Midhurst - Branch Lines around A 49 5
Midhurst - Branch Lines to A 01 0 OOP
Military Defence of West Sussex A 23 1
Military Signals, South Coast C 54 0
Minehead - Branch Line to A 80 0
Mitcham Junction Lines B 01 4
Mitchell & company C 59 1
Moreton-in-Marsh to Worcester D 26 8
Moretonhampstead - Branch Line to C 27 3
N
Newbury to Westbury C 66 4
Newport - Branch Lines to A 26 6
Newquay - Branch Lines to C 71 0
Newton Abbot to Plymouth C 60 5
Northern France Narrow Gauge C 75 3
North East German Narrow Gauge D 44 6
North Kent Tramways B 44 8
North London Line B 94 4
North Woolwich - BLs around C 65 6
Norwich Tramways C 40 0
Notts & Derby Tramway D 53 5
O
Orpington to Tonbridge B 03 0
Oxford to Moreton-in-Marsh D 15 2
P
Paddington to Ealing C 37 0
Paddington to Princes Risborough C 81 8
Padstow - Branch Line to B 54 5
Plymouth - BLs around B 98 7
Plymouth to St. Austell C 63 X
Porthmadog 1954-94 - BL around B 31 6
Porthmadog to Blaenau B 50 2 OOP
Portmadoc 1923-46 - BL around B 13 8
Portsmouths Tramways B 72 3 OOP
Portsmouth to Southampton A 31 2
Portsmouth Trolleybuses C 73 7
Princes Risborough - Branch Lines to D 05 5
Princes Risborough to Banbury C 85 0
R
Railways to Victory C 16 8 OOP
Reading to Basingstoke B 27 8
Reading to Didcot C 79 6
Reading to Guildford A 47 9 OOP
Reading Tramways B 87 1
Reading Trolleybuses C 05 2
Redhill to Ashford A 73 8
Return to Blaenau 1970-82 C 64 8
Roman Roads of Surrey C 61 3
Roman Roads of Sussex C 48 6
Romneyrail C 32 X
Ryde to Ventnor A 19 3
S
Salisbury to Westbury B 39 1
Salisbury to Yeovil B 06 5
Saxmundham to Yarmouth C 69 9
Saxony Narrow Gauge D 47 0
Seaton & Eastbourne T/Ws B 76 6 OOP
Seaton & Sidmouth - Branch Lines to A 95 9
Secret Sussex Resistance B 82 0
SECR Centenary album C 11 7
Selsey - Branch Line to A 04 5 OOP
Sheerness - Branch Lines around B 16 2
Shepherds Bush to Uxbridge T/Ws C 28 1
Shrewsbury - Branch Line to A 86 X
Sierra Leone Narrow Gauge D 28 4
Sittingbourne to Ramsgate A 90 8
Slough to Newbury C 56 7
Solent - Creeks, Crafts & Cargoes D 52 7
Southamptons Tramways B 33 2 OOP

Southampton to Bournemouth A 42 8
Southend-on-Sea Tramways B 28 6
Southern France Narrow Gauge C 47 8
Southwark & Deptford Tramways B 38 3
Southwold - Branch Line to A 15 0
South Eastern & Chatham Railways C 08
South London Line B 46 4
South London Tramways 1903-33 D 10 1
St. Albans to Bedford D 08 X
St. Austell to Penzance C 67 2
St. Pancras to St. Albans C 78 8
Stamford Hill Tramways B 85 5
Steaming through Cornwall B 30 8
Steaming through East Cornwall B 30 8
Steaming through Kent A 13 4 OOP
Steaming through the Isle of Wight A 56 8
Steaming through West Hants A 69 X
Stratford-upon-Avon to Cheltenham C 25
Strood to Paddock Wood B 12 X
Surrey Home Guard C 57 5
Surrey Narrow Gauge C 87 7
Surrey Waterways A 51 7 OOP
Sussex Home Guard C 24 9
Sussex Narrow Gauge C 68 0
Sussex Shipping Sail, Steam & Motor D 23 3
Swanley to Ashford B 45 6
Swindon to Bristol C 96 6
Swindon to Gloucester D46 2
Swindon to Newport D 30 6
Swiss Narrow Gauge C 94 X
T
Talyllyn - 50 years C 39 7
Taunton to Barnstaple B 60 X
Taunton to Exeter C 82 6
Tavistock to Plymouth B 88 X
Tenterden - Branch Line to A 21 5
Thanet's Tramways B 11 1 OOP
Three Bridges to Brighton A 35 5
Tilbury Loop C 86 9
Tiverton - Branch Lines around C 62 1
Tivetshall to Beccles D 41 1
Tonbridge to Hastings A 44 4
Torrington - Branch Lines to B 37 5
Tunbridge Wells - Branch Lines to A 32 0
Twickenham & Kingston Trys C 35 4
Two-Foot Gauge Survivors C 21 4 OOP
U
Upwell - Branch Line to B 64 2
V
Victoria & Lambeth Tramways B 49 9
Victoria to Bromley South A 98 3
Victoria to East Croydon A 40 1
Vivarais C 31 1
W
Walthamstow & Leyton Tramways B 65 0
Waltham Cross & Edmonton Trys C 07 9
Wandsworth & Battersea Tramways B 63
Wantage - Branch Line to D 25 X
Wareham to Swanage - 50 yrs D 09 8
War on the Line A 10 X
War on the Line VIDEO + 88 0
Waterloo to Windsor A 54 1
Waterloo to Woking A 38 X
Watford to Leighton Buzzard D 45 4
Wenford Bridge to Fowey C 09 5
Westbury to Bath B 55 3
Westbury to Taunton C 76 1
West Cornwall Mineral Railways D 48 9
West Croydon to Epsom B 08 1
West London - Branch Lines of C 50 8
West London Line B 84 7
West Sussex Waterways A 24 X
West Wiltshire - Branch Lines of D 12 8
Weymouth - Branch Lines around A 65 7
Willesden Junction to Richmond B 71 5
Wimbledon to Beckenham C 58 3
Wimbledon to Epsom B 62 6
Wimborne - Branch Lines around A 97 5
Wisbech - Branch Lines around C 01 X
Wisbech 1800-1901 C 93 1
Woking to Alton A 59 2
Woking to Portsmouth A 25 8
Woking to Southampton A 55 X
Woolwich & Dartford Trolleys B 66 9 OOP*
Worcester to Hereford D 38 1
Worthing to Chichester A 06 1 OOP
Y
Yeovil - 50 yrs change C 38 9
Yeovil to Dorchester A 76 2
Yeovil to Exeter A 91 6

CONTENTS

04-05 WHAT IS A GOGO°?

06-09 GOGO'S PROFILES 01 - 32

10-11 GAME RULES — BASEBALL · CRAZY TOUCH · BATTLE

12-17 GOGO'S PROFILES 33 - 80

18 DOC'S DATA CHECK

19 @BONE TEASERS! WACKY WORDS

20-21 @BONE TEASERS! GOGO° CHAOS · LOST GOGO'S°

22-25 EVOLUTION GOGO'S PROFILES 01 - 32

26 THE XAR & NASOKI SHOW

27 DOC'S DATA CHECK

28-31 EVOLUTION GOGO'S PROFILES 33 - 64

32-33 GAME RULES — BASKET · SCORING

34-35 EVOLUTION GOGO'S PROFILES 65 - 80

36-37 @BONE TEASERS! WORD CROSS · JIGSAW JUMBLE

38-41 EXPLORER GOGO'S PROFILES 01 - 32

42 DOC'S DATA CHECK

43 @BONE TEASERS! FAWA'S PHOTOS!

44-45 @BONE TEASERS! DOODLE-A-GOGO°! · SATORI'S SPOT-IT

46-51 EXPLORER GOGO'S PROFILES 33 - 80

52-53 GAME RULES — BooFlip · In flight · BOWLING

54-55 GOGO'S CRAZY BONES CHECKLIST

56-57 EVOLUTION GOGO'S CRAZY BONES CHECKLIST

58-59 EXPLORER GOGO'S CRAZY BONES CHECKLIST

60-63 @BONE TEASERS! ANSWERS

WHAT IS A GOGO®?

As soon as you put a Gogo in your hand, you'll see why it is so original. Each Gogo's face, shape and colouring are unique.

But there are lots more things you need to know about the Gogo's. Learn how to spot an original series from Evolution or Explorer.

Learn everything you can about the original Gogo's and tackling the later ones will come with ease.

NAME AND NUMBER
Every Gogo has a name and number. You'll find all their names in this annual. If you look closely at the back of your Gogo, you'll find its number printed just above the MAGIC BOX INT. stamp.

GOGO PERSONALITIES
Each Gogo is very special and has its own personality and special abilities. If you want to know more about them, you can read their profiles right here in this annual. You'll also find information on each of the Gogo's favourite games.

SKILLS BAR

SKILLS:

SPEED: This shows whether the Gogo will gain speed and crash strength.

BOUNCE: This tells you whether it is easy to predict where the Gogo will land after it's thrown or whether it is likely to fly off in a direction you didn't expect.

BALANCE: This shows the likelihood of the Gogo standing up when it is thrown – remember a standing Gogo gets a much higher score.

01 MOSH
Super kind. All the Gogo's want to be friends with Mosh.
SPECIAL ABILITY:
Magic Smile
FAVOURITE GAME: K.O.

SKILLS:

01 MOSH
Super kind. All the Gogo's want to be friends with Mosh.
SPECIAL ABILITY:
Magic Smile
FAVOURITE GAME: **K.O.**

SPECIAL ABILITY
All the Gogo's have a special ability that is unique to them which they use to their best advantage.

FAVOURITE GAME
This indicates the game that the Gogo usually performs best in.

EVOLUTION gogo's CRAZY BONES

The Gogo's have evolved new characters, new skills and new things for you to look out for.

MOSHI 01
Avoids confrontation. Always brings goodness and peace.
SPECIAL ABILITY: Peacemaker
EVOLUTION: 15
FAVOURITE GAME: K.O.

EVOLUTION BAR
Gogo's have EVOLVED! Use the EVOLUTION BAR to see how much each character has evolved.

LEVEL 15 = MAXIMUM EVOLUTION
LEVEL 1 = MINIMUM EVOLUTION

TRANSPARENT EVOLUTION
You can recognize the Gogo's with TRANSPARENT EVOLUTION by this symbol.

EXPLORER gogo's CRAZY BONES

Gogo's are everywhere, with new features, new characters and a whole new world of Gogo's for you to explore.

01 FLAMER
Keeps the other Gogos warm, even in the coldest places.
SPECIAL ABILITY: Chimney Mouth
FAVOURITE GAME: Basket

LASER COLOUR
Apart from the 4 normal colours, each Gogo is available in LASER COLOUR, which is easily identified because of its amazing shiny effect.

EXPLORATION FEATURES
These are a series of features that indicate each Gogo's exploring abilities.

 The Gogo's with this symbol move very well in cities, either on the streets or inside houses and buildings.
Many Gogo's prefer to explore places away from the city, like forests, beaches... even deserts.
Some Gogo's are daring enough to investigate the world of water, from a small bath to the amazing seabed.

 There are also some air specialists who know how to fly or understand the climate, wind and clouds.
The Gogo's with this symbol like to explore small, and often hidden, secret places.
If your Gogo has this symbol, it means that it has the ability to move very freely and often travels large distances.
The compass symbol indicates that the Gogo has a good sense of direction, which stops it from getting lost and helps it to find the best route for reaching any destination.

HOW TO PLAY
You'll never be bored with a Gogo; there are so many games to play! Different Gogo's are better for playing different games depending on their size, shape and weight. Check out the profiles and use the handy guide to find out which games will best suit your Gogo's.

THE BACK
Look on the back of your Gogo's and you'll find they are all designed the same so that you can hold them or throw them with just one finger. Of course, practise is the key to becoming a Gogo champion.

COLOURS
Each Gogo is available in five different colours. All the colours of every Gogo can be found at the back of the annual in the checklist section.

DON'T ACCEPT ANY IMITATIONS
Pick up a Gogo and turn it over to check that it has the MAGIC BOX INT. stamp. The MAGIC BOX INT. stamp guarantees that your Gogo is an original, has a fantastic bounce and is a bright, shiny colour.

PROFILES

01 MOSH

Super kind. All the Gogo's want to be friends with Mosh.

SPECIAL ABILITY:
Magic Smile

FAVOURITE GAME: K.O.

SKILLS:

NASAKO 02

Always cool because he has a special scoring technique.

SPECIAL ABILITY:
Double Fast Hook

FAVOURITE GAME: Battle

SKILLS:

SATO 03

Ready for the fight. Where's the ring?

SPECIAL ABILITY:
K.O. Punch

FAVOURITE GAME: Battle

SKILLS:

04 OKORI

Nobody knows what he eats, but whatever it is, it isn't doing him any good.

SPECIAL ABILITY:
Eating

FAVOURITE GAME: Scoring

SKILLS:

TORI 05

Clever and fun, he likes to be the boss.

SPECIAL ABILITY:
Jumps Walls

FAVOURITE GAME: Scoring

SKILLS:

06 HELLY

The fastest Gogo. His helmet helps him to go breathtakingly fast.

SPECIAL ABILITY:
Continuous Sprint

FAVOURITE GAME: On Line

SKILLS:

08+08 ANGIRU

Tell Angiru your secrets and they will be safe for ever.

SPECIAL ABILITY:
Keeps Secrets

FAVOURITE GAME: Basket

SKILLS:

SKULL 07

He looks mysterious and when you least expect it, he'll do something funny to make you jump.

SPECIAL ABILITY:
Spooky Skills

FAVOURITE GAME: Basket

SKILLS:

PROFILES

UMU 09 ♂

Likes to visit the swimming pool every day to think up new ideas.

SPECIAL ABILITY : **Intelligent Swimming**

FAVOURITE GAME: **In Flight**

AIKO 10 ♀

The Gogo with the best sense of smell. Can detect a smell from a mile away.

SPECIAL ABILITY : **Wonder Nose**

FAVOURITE GAME: **In Flight**

ICHIRO 11 + 11S ♂

Don't stare into its eyes. You'll be overcome by its great mental power.

SPECIAL ABILITY : **Dagger Eyes**

FAVOURITE GAME: **Bowling**

12 NUCLOS ♂

Absorbs pollution and leaves the air really clean.

SPECIAL ABILITY : **Pollution Reduction**

FAVOURITE GAME: **K.O.**

13 BOY ♂

The best blindfolded runner. He never falls over.

SPECIAL ABILITY : **Sensory Space Radar**

FAVOURITE GAME: **Basket**

NEKO 14 ♂

Uses his body to protect the other Gogo's from fire.

SPECIAL ABILITY : **Flame Catcher**

FAVOURITE GAME: **On Line**

15 HAZARD ♂

When faced with danger, it just grits its teeth and carries on.

SPECIAL ABILITY : **Courage**

FAVOURITE GAME: **K.O.**

16 SUN ♂

Fires a ray of optimism at every Gogo in its path.

SPECIAL ABILITY : **Happy Ray**

FAVOURITE GAME: **K.O.**

SKILLS:

PROFILES

HIRO 17

Solves problems with electrifying 500W ideas.

SPECIAL ABILITY: Electric Ideas

FAVOURITE GAME: In Flight

SKILLS:

18 AKA

Can collide with 100 Gogo's without getting any bumps or bruises.

SPECIAL ABILITY: Hammer Head

FAVOURITE GAME: Bowling

SKILLS:

MOLLY 19

Getting angry is no problem because it lasts less than a second.

SPECIAL ABILITY: Micro-Anger

FAVOURITE GAME: K.O.

SKILLS:

NARI 20

Don't try to stare out Nari - you will lose.

SPECIAL ABILITY: Concentration

FAVOURITE GAME: In Flight

SKILLS:

21 SIMI

Smiling charges up his powers. He smiles and then shoots away.

SPECIAL ABILITY: Power Smiles

FAVOURITE GAME: Battle

SKILLS:

CODI 22

Always connected. Ask it anything and the data will be downloaded.

SPECIAL ABILITY: Quick Connection

FAVOURITE GAME: In Flight

SKILLS:

23 HIRAKU

The most daring pirate - endless adventures.

SPECIAL ABILITY: Boarding

FAVOURITE GAME: Bowling

SKILLS:

RUFUS 24

Sees things others can't using the powers of Planet X.

SPECIAL ABILITY: X-Vision

FAVOURITE GAME: In Flight

SKILLS:

08

PROFILES

TEMP 25

Is the water really cold? What time is it going to rain? Just ask Temp.

SPECIAL ABILITY: **Weather Forecasting**

FAVOURITE GAME: On Line

SKILLS:

PIBI 26

Organizes ideas in both sides of its head. Need ideas, speak to Pibi.

SPECIAL ABILITY: **Double Brain**

FAVOURITE GAME: Basket

SKILLS:

27 DARE

The best-looking Gogo. He always looks his best.

SPECIAL ABILITY: **Photogenic**

FAVOURITE GAME: Battle

SKILLS:

DANKO 28

Feline, fast, agile and well-behaved.

SPECIAL ABILITY: **Cute and Cuddly**

FAVOURITE GAME: Bowling

SKILLS:

30 GAIJI

Takes control of the situation. An expert in crowd control.

SPECIAL ABILITY: **Battle Helmet**

FAVOURITE GAME: Battle

SKILLS:

29 MC TOY

Always careful and questioning. Never makes a wrong move.

SPECIAL ABILITY: **No Mistakes**

FAVOURITE GAME: In Flight

SKILLS:

31 LESSI

Sometimes feels a little low. You might need to perk him up.

SPECIAL ABILITY: **Shock-Absorber**

FAVOURITE GAME: K.O.

SKILLS:

32 POP

Loves music and dances non-stop.

SPECIAL ABILITY: **Top Rhythm**

FAVOURITE GAME: On Line

SKILLS:

GAME RULES

BATTLE

① Two players arrange six or more of their Gogo's in parallel rows a short distance apart.

② Players must decide before the start of the match how many throws there will be.

③ Players then throw their Gogo at their opponent's row and attempt to knock Gogo's out of the line.

④ The player who knocks down the most of their opponent's Gogo's wins.

TIPS

If using basic rules, the Gogo's do not need to fall over completely, but simply be knocked out of the line.

If you want to play advanced rules, then the Gogo's must actually be knocked over as well as being pushed out of the line.

CRAZY TOUCH

① Take a box – a shoebox will do – and place at least 10 Gogo's inside.

② Each player takes turns to reach into the box with their eyes covered and pick up a Gogo.

① Draw a baseball diamond on the ground. Decide who will be 'batter' and place that player's Gogo on the batting plate.

② That player then rolls four Gogo's and works out how far to move their Gogo using the score card below.

③ The player moves the Gogo's around the diamond the required number of spaces. Each time a Gogo makes a complete circuit of the diamond the player scores a point.

SCORE CARD

X1	HOME RUN	=	1 POINT
X4	HOME RUN	=	1 POINT
X3	TRIPLE	=	MOVE 3 BASES
X2	DOUBLE	=	MOVE 2 BASES
X1	SINGLE	=	MOVE 1 BASE
X0	ZERO	=	BATTER IS OUT!

④ When the batter is out three times it is the other player's turn. The game can go on for any number of rounds, but the traditional number for a baseball game is nine. The winner is the player with the most points at the end of the game.

③ With their eyes still covered, the player must guess which Gogo they have in their hand by feeling it. A correct guess scores a point. The first player to get 10 points wins.

④ Give the box a shake between turns to mix the Gogo's up.

TIP

If you want to make the game even more difficult, the first player to get 10 points in a row wins.

PROFILES

33 IMON

Absorbs ideas through its star.

SPECIAL ABILITY:
Mental Strength

FAVOURITE GAME: Battle

SKILLS:

34 JELLY

Brave enough for any battle.

SPECIAL ABILITY:
Super Warrior

FAVOURITE GAME: Battle

SKILLS:

SUMON 35

Traps his enemies inside his huge powerful jaws.

SPECIAL ABILITY:
Mouth-Cage

FAVOURITE GAME: Bowling

SKILLS:

36 CHO

Races ahead at full speed – that's why he doesn't have any teeth left.

SPECIAL ABILITY:
Energy

FAVOURITE GAME: Battle

SKILLS:

RAYSUN 37

Has a great time bringing sunshine into the Gogo's world.

SPECIAL ABILITY:
Sun Ray

FAVOURITE GAME: Bowling

SKILLS:

38 + 38 S FIST

Holds a secret strength inside his fist.

SPECIAL ABILITY:
Ultimate Grip

FAVOURITE GAME: Basket

SKILLS:

40 HAYATO

Wants 20 mirrors nearby to keep an eye on everything.

SPECIAL ABILITY:
Super Wink

FAVOURITE GAME: Basket

SKILLS:

ZAR-ZAR 39

Pretends not to understand but knows much more than you think.

SPECIAL ABILITY:
Cunning

FAVOURITE GAME: Basket

SKILLS:

PROFILES

BIGU 41

Stands tall and upright.
Gives fun orders to the troops.

SPECIAL ABILITY:
Fun Orders

FAVOURITE GAME: K.O.

SKILLS:

OJARU 42

Badly sewn together
but strong enough to know
the secret of flight.

SPECIAL ABILITY:
Flying Ears

FAVOURITE GAME: In Flight

SKILLS:

43 SPEED

Turns his head with supersonic
speed and always sees the
world around him.

SPECIAL ABILITY:
Panoramic View

FAVOURITE GAME: On Line

SKILLS:

44 TREMI

Appearances can be deceptive.
Not as grumpy as he looks.

SPECIAL ABILITY:
Laughter Mask

FAVOURITE GAME: Battle

SKILLS:

45 # 45 S B-BOY

Eats a lot of popcorn to improve
his bouncing power.

SPECIAL ABILITY:
Popcorn Attack

FAVOURITE GAME: Basket

SKILLS:

MOCHI 46

A lucky charm amongst the
Gogo's family.

SPECIAL ABILITY:
Lucky Power

FAVOURITE GAME: On Line

SKILLS:

POPUS 47

Digs long tunnels to
move around without anyone
knowing he is there.

SPECIAL ABILITY:
Earth Eater

FAVOURITE GAME: Bowling

SKILLS:

48 TUBE

Thanks to gramophone
ears, it hears everything
and can play it all back.

SPECIAL ABILITY:
Rec and Play

FAVOURITE GAME: On Line

SKILLS:

PROFILES

CUBIC 49

A robot Gogo who is an expert mechanic.

SPECIAL ABILITY:
Repairs Everything

FAVOURITE GAME: K.O.

B-KING 50

When he sits down to think, he acts like a tribal chief.

SPECIAL ABILITY:
Magic Horns

FAVOURITE GAME: Battle

CROC 51

Croc is a chequered crocodile. In other words, a crocodile chess master.

SPECIAL ABILITY:
Check Mate

FAVOURITE GAME: Scoring

52 UFUS

With its rubber Ninja body, it can fly long distances between bounces.

SPECIAL ABILITY:
Flying Bounce

FAVOURITE GAME: Scoring

53 EGBOT

Communicates through waves, thanks to its electromagnetic mouth.

SPECIAL ABILITY:
Electric Jump

FAVOURITE GAME: Basket

H-83 54

A strong shell makes it super-resistant.

SPECIAL ABILITY:
Throws Stars

FAVOURITE GAME: K.O.

ATORI 55

Keeps all its knowledge safe inside and then closes the zip.

SPECIAL ABILITY:
Giga Memory

FAVOURITE GAME: K.O.

B-BALL 56

If the sport has a ball, he is the master.

SPECIAL ABILITY:
Ball Skills

FAVOURITE GAME: Basket

14

PROFILES

USUZI 57

If something goes wrong, he is very nervous until a solution is found.

SPECIAL ABILITY:
Clamp Click

FAVOURITE GAME: **Battle**

SKILLS:

58 ECO

Can travel over any obstacle or difficult terrain using four arms.

SPECIAL ABILITY:
4x4 Race

FAVOURITE GAME: **Basket**

SKILLS:

OH! 59

Loves to surprise all the other Gogo's.

SPECIAL ABILITY:
Hiding

FAVOURITE GAME: **In Flight**

SKILLS:

ALKALINE 60

Ultra turbo-charged power. Full blast energy.

SPECIAL ABILITY:
Battery Charger

FAVOURITE GAME: **Battle**

SKILLS:

61 AWA-SHIMA

Always ready for action, but don't bother him for anything else.

SPECIAL ABILITY:
Graffiti-Flash

FAVOURITE GAME: **K.O.**

SKILLS:

62 GHOST

Dark mystery. Not everyone dares look him in the face.

SPECIAL ABILITY:
Frightening Whisper

FAVOURITE GAME: **Basket**

SKILLS:

SKILLS:

63 TUT

The curious mummy. Can remove a tiny bit of bandage to see what is going on.

SPECIAL ABILITY:
Healing

FAVOURITE GAME: **K.O.**

MATSUE 64

Very proud of his super-cool haircut.

SPECIAL ABILITY:
Soft Fringe

FAVOURITE GAME: **In Flight**

SKILLS:

15

PROFILES

65 AKITA

Friend and loyal companion.
You can count on Akita.

SPECIAL ABILITY:
Antenna Horn

FAVOURITE GAME: On Line

SKILLS:

SHIZUOKA 66

With just one cry he can get the
attention of all the Gogo's.

SPECIAL ABILITY:
Gogo's Alert

FAVOURITE GAME: K.O.

SKILLS:

MIYAKE 67

Cuts through water at
amazing speed.

SPECIAL ABILITY:
Rudder Shaped Crest

FAVOURITE GAME: On Line

SKILLS:

68 FUJICHIK

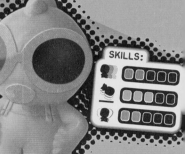

Flies fast and high,
but lands soft and smooth.

SPECIAL ABILITY:
Instant Landing

FAVOURITE GAME: In Flight

SKILLS:

TSU 69

Juices, cold drinks,
he always has a drink handy.
A thirsty Gogo.

SPECIAL ABILITY:
Big Gulp

FAVOURITE GAME: Bowling

SKILLS:

70 KOKUBU

The life and soul of any party.
Invited to every occasion.

SPECIAL ABILITY:
Friend Visor

FAVOURITE GAME: Bowling

SKILLS:

IZUMI 71

Loves speed and never gets off
his motorbike.

SPECIAL ABILITY:
Motorbike Racing

FAVOURITE GAME: On Line

SKILLS:

72 AKO

The ultimate minder.
50 special moves ready to go.

SPECIAL ABILITY:
Martial Arts

FAVOURITE GAME: Battle

SKILLS:

PROFILES

KAMI-KAMI 73

Brushes his teeth before playing any game. Always fresh and minty.

SPECIAL ABILITY: **Super Bite**

FAVOURITE GAME: **Scoring**

SKILLS:

SAGO 74

Changes shape to fit into any space.

SPECIAL ABILITY: **Self-Moulding**

FAVOURITE GAME: **Scoring**

SKILLS:

VAMPA 75

Not seen much during the day. He moves in the dark.

SPECIAL ABILITY: **Low-Level Flying**

FAVOURITE GAME: **Scoring**

SKILLS:

76 MISHA

Cute and cuddly, the best sleeping companion around.

SPECIAL ABILITY: **Makes You Sleepy**

FAVOURITE GAME: **Scoring**

SKILLS:

77 YUZA

As strong as a rock. Arms like granite.

SPECIAL ABILITY: **Weight Lifting**

FAVOURITE GAME: **K.O.**

SKILLS:

TAN CHIA 78

Wants to be the Gogo's hero. Always ready for action.

SPECIAL ABILITY: **Free Fighting**

FAVOURITE GAME: **Battle**

SKILLS:

79 KOLO

Futuristic Gogo who loves technology. Floats through space guided by the stars.

SPECIAL ABILITY: **Space Flight**

FAVOURITE GAME: **Bowling**

SKILLS:

80 EVI

Although it tries to frighten its friends, it makes them laugh more than anything.

SPECIAL ABILITY: **Attack of Laughter**

FAVOURITE GAME: **In Flight**

SKILLS:

DOC'S DATA CHECK

1 Which of these Gogo's does not have a transparent evolution?

A. Yonozi ☐

B. Sut ☐

C. Sip ☐

2 Which Gogo likes to get to the front of the queue and give the other Gogo's something to aim for?

_____

3 If Zhip's number is taken away from Lucky Rab's, what is left?

A. 28 ☐

B. 7 ☐

C. 43 ☐

4 Which Gogo wears this logo?

_____

5 Can you untangle the name of the Gogo below?

Y	N	U	R	A	S
☐	☐	☐	☐	☐	☐

6 Which Gogo sometimes needs perking up?

A. Dare ☐

B. Lessi ☐

C. Danko ☐

7 Can you name the two Gogo's who have got into a bit of a mix-up here?

A. _____

B. _____

FIND ALL THE ANSWERS ON PAGE 60

Can you find all the Gogo's hiding in this jumble of letters?

Use the list below to help you find all their names.

```
          C U G Y F
      M B U J A J S B        A
    A K I P Q N   M T A     L
  L K V R I X N     Z A   R K
M L O P T X N C   A F   U B A K E M
 A A N S U D H A C A L D B J O L A I K
T A T E R R W A V S G Y O I R   H Z
 N T G W P M A H I D   I E O K C O N   V
J Q U H O W L X   G H G L R U R C E N H B E O
E Z E   C I N I H E L R U R   A G Q O Z   Q I R
 E W N   T H L D T R W J E J U   A R P E Z I K R
E   F K L T A B O E M G A I S O Y A K E V I F
 T   N O R N V N O G L E A M I   U E D Q
      F B N L                     H C
        B S
```

Word List

- [ ] Aiko
- [ ] Alkaline
- [ ] Angiru
- [ ] Akone
- [ ] Boki
- [ ] Birtu
- [ ] Champer
- [ ] Cupix
- [ ] Chiru
- [ ] Enko
- [ ] Fujichik
- [ ] Gaisor
- [ ] Gondo
- [ ] Hilbo
- [ ] Matsue
- [ ] Miyake
- [ ] Nuchan
- [ ] Starboro
- [ ] Switel
- [ ] Yonozi

It's chaos in Gogo's world! Can you help sort out the mess the unsupervised Gogo's have got themselves into? Before they can get on with their games the Gogo's need to know just how many of them there are.

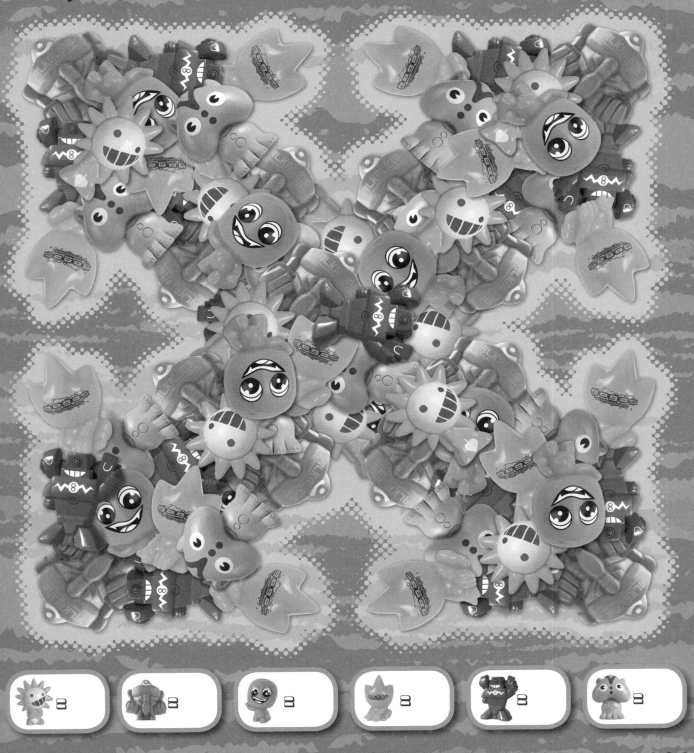

LOST GOGO'S®

The Gogo's Explorers love nothing better than an adventure, and after receiving a letter from their other Gogo pals they can't wait to meet up with them.

If only they could find a way to their friends. Can you help?

START

FINISH

21

PROFILES

MOSHI 01
Avoids confrontation. Always brings goodness and peace.

SPECIAL ABILITY:
Peacemaker

FAVOURITE GAME: K.O.

EVOLUTION: 15

02 NASOKI
Tries to make everyone laugh. Sometimes his looks scare the others a little bit.

SPECIAL ABILITY:
Joker

FAVOURITE GAME: Bowling

EVOLUTION: 11

03 SATORI
Always watchful in case action is needed.

SPECIAL ABILITY:
Watchful Eye

FAVOURITE GAME: Basket

EVOLUTION: 12

OKY 04
Maybe some indigestion gave him a mushroom face.

SPECIAL ABILITY:
Fungus Fury

FAVOURITE GAME: Bowling

EVOLUTION: 13

05 RACETOR
He loves sports and can calculate how to win any race.

SPECIAL ABILITY:
Numeric Memory

FAVOURITE GAME: Scoring

EVOLUTION: 09

HELED 06
He robotized his brain to think super fast.

SPECIAL ABILITY:
Mental Dexterity

FAVOURITE GAME: K.O.

EVOLUTION: 08

07 SKER
He's naive and everything seems weird to him.

SPECIAL ABILITY:
Curiosity

FAVOURITE GAME: In Flight

EVOLUTION: 10

08 ANGOR
Night mysteries are no secret to Angor.

SPECIAL ABILITY:
Insomnia

FAVOURITE GAME: In Flight

EVOLUTION: 06

PROFILES

TAI-UMU 09

With the points of his mouth-star he chews the hardest things.

SPECIAL ABILITY:
Star Scream

FAVOURITE GAME: Bowling

EVOLUTION: 13

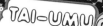

KOKU-CHAN 10

He must go to the barber every day because his hair grows while he plays.

SPECIAL ABILITY:
Manic Hair

FAVOURITE GAME: In Flight

EVOLUTION: 13

11 CHIRU

The moon reflects in his eyes when he's sleepy.

SPECIAL ABILITY:
Counting Sheep

FAVOURITE GAME: Basket

EVOLUTION: 08

NUCHAN 12

Serious and thoughtful. He acts like the chief Gogo.

SPECIAL ABILITY:
Action Planning

FAVOURITE GAME: On Line

EVOLUTION: 11

OM-POH 13

Uses spells to play better. Sometimes it works.

SPECIAL ABILITY:
Multiple Faces

FAVOURITE GAME: Battle

EVOLUTION: 10

14 NEBUB

Concentrates the water supply to put out any fire.

SPECIAL ABILITY:
Firefighting

FAVOURITE GAME: On Line

EVOLUTION: 09

HAZER 15

His game style is funny and he goes crazy watching others play.

SPECIAL ABILITY:
Unintentional Humour

FAVOURITE GAME: Battle

EVOLUTION: 11

SUNON 16

Ticklish all over his body. Nobody can even stand close to him.

SPECIAL ABILITY:
Ticklish

FAVOURITE GAME: Battle

EVOLUTION: 12

PROFILES

17 HIROKI
Never afraid of new games. Always on the front line.

SPECIAL ABILITY: Bravery

FAVOURITE GAME: On Line

EVOLUTION: 14

AKONE 18
The masters made him into a Kung Fu hero.

SPECIAL ABILITY: Invisible Karate Chop

FAVOURITE GAME: Scoring

EVOLUTION: 13

19 SULLY
The energy of the stars is always with him. . . or so he says.

SPECIAL ABILITY: Force Concentrator

FAVOURITE GAME: Basket

EVOLUTION: 10

NARION 20
He shows himself in darkness thanks to his glowing glasses.

SPECIAL ABILITY: Particle Searcher

FAVOURITE GAME: Battle

EVOLUTION: 08

SIMSEI 21
His mouth acts like a freezer and he's always shivering.

SPECIAL ABILITY: Walking Freezer

FAVOURITE GAME: Basket

EVOLUTION: 04

22 DOKI
He has an incredibly sweet tooth. When he's not playing he's hunting for sweets.

SPECIAL ABILITY: Sweet Gobbler

FAVOURITE GAME: Basket

EVOLUTION: 12

23 HIRCHAN
No hook and no eye-patch but this pirate is still sailing the high seas.

SPECIAL ABILITY: Treasure Finder

FAVOURITE GAME: Scoring

EVOLUTION: 05

24 RUFISTAR
He's the main attraction at any party. Creates fun for everyone.

SPECIAL ABILITY: Hell Raiser

FAVOURITE GAME: Battle

EVOLUTION: 11

PROFILES

EVOLUTION gogo's
CRAZY BONES

25 TEMSEI

He's a real handyman. He can fix anything. . . except his own shoelaces!

SPECIAL ABILITY:
Fixer Fantastic

FAVOURITE GAME: Scoring

EVOLUTION: 11

PILHY 26

He's got a positive pole, a negative pole and he's fully charged.

SPECIAL ABILITY:
Electric Play

FAVOURITE GAME: In Flight

EVOLUTION: 14

DORO 27

Restless and playful. He gets nervous when nobody plays.

SPECIAL ABILITY:
Valiant Ideas

FAVOURITE GAME: Basket

EVOLUTION: 10

28 DANOKI

Loves to lurk around corners and hide from others.

SPECIAL ABILITY:
Camouflage

FAVOURITE GAME: In Flight

EVOLUTION: 12

29 MC-MASK

His head is always in the clouds. He's a dreamer.

SPECIAL ABILITY:
Imagination

FAVOURITE GAME: On Line

EVOLUTION: 09

GAISOR 30

Firm and fair. He likes to be in command of every situation.

SPECIAL ABILITY:
Laser Order

FAVOURITE GAME: Battle

EVOLUTION: 10

LESSEI 31

Moves his head to the rhythm of any music.

SPECIAL ABILITY:
Rotating Neck

FAVOURITE GAME: K.O.

EVOLUTION: 15

32 POPO

Doesn't like too many bumps but with his lucky star he is a very skilful player.

SPECIAL ABILITY:
Lucky Star

FAVOURITE GAME: Bowling

EVOLUTION: 12

THE XAR & NASOKI SHOW

Why are pirates so mean?

I don't know, they just **ARRRRe!**

What happened to the cat that swallowed a ball of wool?

She had mittens!

What do you get if you cross a ghost with a boy scout?

Someone who frightens old ladies across the road!

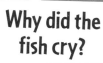

Why did the fish cry?

Because the seaweed!

What did the lion say when he saw the boy go past on his skateboard?

Meals on Wheels!

Why didn't the skeleton go to the movies?

Because he had no body to go with!

DOC'S DATA CHECK

1 Which of these Gogo's is not available in a special edition?

A. Fist ☐

B. Cubic ☐

C. B-Boy ☐

2 I have an evolution number of 11, I love to play Basket and I wear headphones. Who am I?

[ ]

3 What is missing from this Gogo?

A. ⊗

B. 🧩

C. ⚡

4 How many eyelashes does E-Flo have?

[ ]

5 Can you name the two Gogo's who have got into a bit of a mix-up here?

A. [ ]

B. [ ]

6 If you saw this, which Gogo would you be looking at?

[ ]

7 Which Gogo wears this mask and why?

[ ]

[ ]

FIND ALL THE ANSWERS ON PAGE 62

PROFILES

IMOOKI 33

A voice in his earphones tells him the rules of every game. He's got such a terrible memory.

SPECIAL ABILITY: Voice Recorder

FAVOURITE GAME: Basket

EVOLUTION: 11

JEZO 34

A long losing streak has made this once confident Gogo suddenly very modest.

SPECIAL ABILITY: Macromodesty

FAVOURITE GAME: Battle

EVOLUTION: 06

SUMI 35

Full of encouragement. Sumi welcomes everyone with open arms.

SPECIAL ABILITY: Hugs

FAVOURITE GAME: Scoring

EVOLUTION: 13

SHOON 36

Evolution has made him safety conscious. He likes to slow everyone down.

SPECIAL ABILITY: Speed Bumps

FAVOURITE GAME: On Line

EVOLUTION: 10

SUNOK 37

Optimistic, happy and calm. Everything in his life is absolutely OK.

SPECIAL ABILITY: Positivity

FAVOURITE GAME: Bowling

EVOLUTION: 08

FIZER 38

Always ready to get the games started.

SPECIAL ABILITY: Ultimate Countdown

FAVOURITE GAME: Basket

EVOLUTION: 07

GAR-GAR 39

Founder of the Gogo's Aerospace Association. Always searching for new horizons.

SPECIAL ABILITY: Galactic Tourist

FAVOURITE GAME: Basket

EVOLUTION: 12

HAYORI 40

Evolution hasn't changed her vanity. Her hair must always be perfect.

SPECIAL ABILITY: Hair Styling

FAVOURITE GAME: Basket

EVOLUTION: 04

PROFILES

EVOLUTION GOGO'S CRAZY BONES

41 MIGU ♂

The tough guy in the troop. He can throw a Gogo higher than anyone else.

SPECIAL ABILITY:
Object Thrower

FAVOURITE GAME: K.O.

EVOLUTION: 08

42 JITTY ♂

Keeps himself cool by flapping his ears.

SPECIAL ABILITY:
Cooling Ears

FAVOURITE GAME: In Flight

EVOLUTION: 11

43 VELOP ♂

He can measure his speed and that of any approaching Gogo.

SPECIAL ABILITY:
Speed Gun

FAVOURITE GAME: On Line

EVOLUTION: 09

44 TRIKE ♂

Very happy with his evolution. He has great pride in himself.

SPECIAL ABILITY:
Crushing Hands

FAVOURITE GAME: Battle

EVOLUTION: 10

45 BOKI ♂

A big tummy and a big appetite. This is one Gogo who is always on time for a meal.

SPECIAL ABILITY:
Potbelllied Punctuality

FAVOURITE GAME: Basket

EVOLUTION: 10

46 CHIMU ♂

Never afraid to get hurt. This is one Gogo who is ready for any daring challenge.

SPECIAL ABILITY:
Rubber Stop

FAVOURITE GAME: On Line

EVOLUTION: 06

47 DUOP ♂

A real split personality. You'd better be careful with how much you trust him.

SPECIAL ABILITY:
Two-Face

FAVOURITE GAME: Bowling

EVOLUTION: 05

48 TUBOR ♂

Always alert and always aware. His senses are even higher when he sleeps.

SPECIAL ABILITY:
Hyper Attention

FAVOURITE GAME: On Line

EVOLUTION: 07

PROFILES

49 CUPIX ♂

Uses his screen face to play Gogo games with his friends.

SPECIAL ABILITY:
Game Player

FAVOURITE GAME: K.O.

EVOLUTION: 08

B-KORI 50 ♂

He's so friendly that his horns don't scare anybody.

SPECIAL ABILITY:
Makes Friends

FAVOURITE GAME: Battle

EVOLUTION: 07

51 CROOKI ♂

An electric shock has left him fully charged.

SPECIAL ABILITY:
Electro-Smile

FAVOURITE GAME: Scoring

EVOLUTION: 06

52 FUSO ♂

A wild dancer. He makes moves that others couldn't even imagine.

SPECIAL ABILITY:
Music Fever

FAVOURITE GAME: Scoring

EVOLUTION: 06

EGOR 53 ♂

The hungriest Gogo of all. Keeps his mouth wide open for instant snacking.

SPECIAL ABILITY:
Ultimate Eating

FAVOURITE GAME: Basket

EVOLUTION: 07

TARI 54 ♂

Never play hide-and-seek with Tari. He wins every time.

SPECIAL ABILITY:
Bionic Eye

FAVOURITE GAME: K.O.

EVOLUTION: 09

EVOLUTION: 10

55 E-FLO ♂

This Gogo loves nature, wildlife and outdoor adventures.

SPECIAL ABILITY:
Exploration

FAVOURITE GAME: K.O.

BALU 56 ♂

He's fascinated by head-to-head challenges. A real thrillseeker.

SPECIAL ABILITY:
Explosive Rivalry

FAVOURITE GAME: Basket

EVOLUTION: 06

57 YONOZI ♂
Likes to get everything arranged in perfect order. Every detail is double checked.

SPECIAL ABILITY: Organization

FAVOURITE GAME: Battle

EVOLUTION: 08

58 EKEN ♂
He's got an anti-bump position which makes him extra hard to tumble down.

SPECIAL ABILITY: Solid Stance

FAVOURITE GAME: Basket

EVOLUTION: 07

♂ KALIN 59
An important Gogo who carries news and information to the others.

SPECIAL ABILITY: Gogo's Representative

FAVOURITE GAME: In Flight

EVOLUTION: 06

60 KINGO ♂
A body that looks like a face, a face that looks like a body. . . some Gogo's don't know what to make of him.

SPECIAL ABILITY: Body-Face

FAVOURITE GAME: Battle

EVOLUTION: 13

FAWA 61 ♂
The official photographer. Always ready to capture a key moment.

SPECIAL ABILITY: Photographic Vision

FAVOURITE GAME: K.O.

EVOLUTION: 06

62 FANTU ♂
When it's time for him to play, he's so happy that his eye starts dancing.

SPECIAL ABILITY: Restless Eye

FAVOURITE GAME: Basket

EVOLUTION: 03

63 TUCOR ♂
A sore loser but really he has a kind heart.

SPECIAL ABILITY: Grumpy Smiles

FAVOURITE GAME: K.O.

EVOLUTION: 08

SUT 64 ♂
Sometimes he walks like a zombie. Sleeping problems maybe?

SPECIAL ABILITY: Zombie Trance

FAVOURITE GAME: In Flight

EVOLUTION: 09

GAME RULES

Basket

1 Take a small cardboard or plastic box.

2 Decide how far from the players the box should be.

K.O.

1 Using a piece of chalk, mark a square (or circle) on the floor.

2 Each player must place the same number of Gogo's inside the square. Decide on the number of throws each player will get.

3 Players take turns to stand two metres away and throw a Gogo into the square in an attempt to knock their opponent's Gogo's out of the square.

4 If a Gogo gets knocked over but not completely out of the square, it can be put back into position, even if it falls on the line.

5 The winner is the player with the most Gogo's left in the square at the end of the agreed number of throws.

GAME RULES

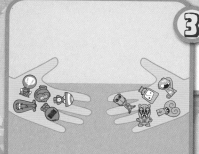

3 Each player picks five Gogo's of the same colour.

4 Take it in turns to throw a Gogo into the box, making sure it bounces before it goes in.

5 The player who gets the most Gogo's into the box is the winner.

SCORING

1 Players choose the number of Gogo's to be used. This can be anything from one to five Gogo's at a time.

2 Each player takes turns to throw their Gogo's on the floor.

EXPLORE A-GOGO!

3 Using the chart below, work out your score by looking at how the Gogo's land.

SCORE CHART

5 POINTS	2 POINTS	1 POINTS	0 POINTS

4 Each player has three goes and the one with the highest score at the end wins. Of course, you can take more turns if you are looking for a longer game!

TAKI 65
Covers his eyes to train his sense of smell. He's always right.
SPECIAL ABILITY: Canine Sense of Smell
FAVOURITE GAME: On Line
EVOLUTION: 10

66 **SKIMY**
He just wants to play games all day long. Never too tired to play.
SPECIAL ABILITY: Happy Smile
FAVOURITE GAME: K.O.
EVOLUTION: 14

67 **KAM**
Obsessed with his music. Talk loudly if you want his attention.
SPECIAL ABILITY: Musical Ear
FAVOURITE GAME: On Line
EVOLUTION: 07

FLICK 68
It's impossible to knock him down if you look straight into his eyes.
SPECIAL ABILITY: Hypnosis
FAVOURITE GAME: In Flight
EVOLUTION: 09

69 **SIP**
Looks like he has bad eyesight but his aim is perfect every time.
SPECIAL ABILITY: Hitting the Target
FAVOURITE GAME: Bowling
EVOLUTION: 06

TRIKU 70
Pays good attention to the game. . . from the front, left and right.
SPECIAL ABILITY: Triple Vision
FAVOURITE GAME: Bowling
EVOLUTION: 07

71 **MIZU**
Locks the target with his eyes and fires straight down the middle.
SPECIAL ABILITY: Mizu Straight Throw
FAVOURITE GAME: On Line
EVOLUTION: 07

72 **VATCO**
Wants to eat something. . . but doesn't know what.
SPECIAL ABILITY: Unknown Appetite
FAVOURITE GAME: Battle
EVOLUTION: 10

34

PROFILES

73 MAKA

A true individual. Happy with his unusual looks.

SPECIAL ABILITY:
Paints Clouds

FAVOURITE GAME: Scoring

EVOLUTION: 14

FEMO 74

He can't wait to join GAR-GAR's Aerospace Association.

SPECIAL ABILITY:
UFO Detector

FAVOURITE GAME: Scoring

EVOLUTION: 13

75 CRUSER

Performs great magic tricks, even though he can't hide anything.

SPECIAL ABILITY:
Transparent Magic Tricks

FAVOURITE GAME: Scoring

EVOLUTION: 08

MISORI 76

Lacking in confidence but always plays better than expected.

SPECIAL ABILITY:
Ear-Antenna

FAVOURITE GAME: Scoring

EVOLUTION: 09

ZUY 77

He thinks that he'll win every game. . . unfortunately, he suffers a lot of disappointment.

SPECIAL ABILITY:
Winning Spirit

FAVOURITE GAME: K.O.

EVOLUTION: 11

78 TIN-CHU

Always proposing some foul play. Loves wrestling.

SPECIAL ABILITY:
Tin-Chu Chop

FAVOURITE GAME: Battle

EVOLUTION: 06

79 SNOK

Spends long hours under water. Everybody goes crazy looking for him.

SPECIAL ABILITY:
Deep Breathing

FAVOURITE GAME: Bowling

EVOLUTION: 12

80 KIVU

Carefully concentrates his thoughts before any attack.

SPECIAL ABILITY:
Concentration

FAVOURITE GAME: In Flight

EVOLUTION: 11

WORD CROSS

Think you know your Gogo's? Are you an expert on Evolution or an egghead on Explorer? Time to test your knowledge with a little teaser.

Don't worry if you're not a Gogo genius – all the answers can be found by looking through this book.

ACROSS

3. This Gogo loves art museums. (5)
4. Likes to visit the swimming pool every day. (3)
6. Which Evolution Gogo's special ability is deep breathing? (4)
8. Which Gogo loves counting sheep? (5)
9. This Gogo is never afraid of new games, and their special ability is bravery. (6)
12. The Gogo that makes everyone laugh. (6)
13. The Gogo's official photographer. (4)
15. This Gogo doesn't wear a muzzle and is good with puzzles. Which Gogo is it? (5)
16. This Gogo's love of sports cars is reflected in its name. (7)

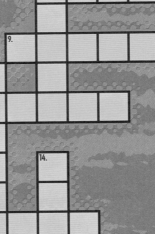

DOWN

1. If you needed a Gogo with a square head which one would you choose? (4)
2. This Gogo is feline, fast and also cute and cuddly. (5)
5. Which Gogo's special ability is Clamp Click? (5)
7. Don't stare into its eyes. (6)
10. This Gogo is known for its chimney mouth. (6)
11. Very proud of its haircut. (6)
14. The amount of points a Gogo scores for landing on its side in Scoring. (3)

JIGSAW JUMBLE

@ BONE TEASERS! #*?

Take a look at the pieces of this broken jigsaw and see if you can see which pieces are missing.

Not all of them fit so make sure you pick the right ones.

A

B

C

D

E

F

G

FIND ALL THE ANSWERS ON PAGE 63

PROFILES

01 FLAMER

Keeps the other Gogo's warm, even in the coldest places.

SPECIAL ABILITY:
Chimney Mouth

FAVOURITE GAME: Basket

EYDO 02

Hides amongst the shadows and discovers secret places.

SPECIAL ABILITY:
Dodges Looks

FAVOURITE GAME: In Flight

TIVI 03

King of the Virtual World – can master a whole load of videogames.

SPECIAL ABILITY:
Screen Jumping

FAVOURITE GAME: Scoring

04 XAR

Goes under water and has the fish laughing their heads off.

SPECIAL ABILITY:
Water Jokes

FAVOURITE GAME: On Line

05 RAYLO

Can find its way around, even if it's pouring with rain.

SPECIAL ABILITY:
Walks Through Storms

FAVOURITE GAME: Battle

TORK 06

Speed and urban sports are its thing. Rollers, skateboards and bikes

SPECIAL ABILITY:
Road Runner

FAVOURITE GAME: Bowling

BIRTU 07

Always dreaming up in the trees with the birds, letting its imagination fly.

SPECIAL ABILITY:
Birdsong

FAVOURITE GAME: In flight

08 MO

Never stops eating, but always keeps fit: joins every expedition!

SPECIAL ABILITY:
Energetic Eating

FAVOURITE GAME: Bowling

PROFILES

ZHIP 09
Has the ability to open just about anything. A popular companion on Gogo expeditions.
SPECIAL ABILITY:
Opens Everything
FAVOURITE GAME: Scoring

10 **ONIKASO**
Never agrees with the routes Eitor proposes, but always tags along.
SPECIAL ABILITY:
Opposite Views
FAVOURITE GAME: Bowling

11 **FANBON**
Likes to appear suddenly in the most unexpected places, like a ghost.
SPECIAL ABILITY:
Happy Music
FAVOURITE GAME: Scoring

JAMPA JAMPA 12
Chooses upward paths, so that it can jump along the route.
SPECIAL ABILITY:
High Jump
FAVOURITE GAME: Bowling

13 **LUNINO**
Gets its bearings easily as it has one eye on each side. That's a real advantage!
SPECIAL ABILITY:
Double Vision
FAVOURITE GAME: In flight

14 **KATO**
Always seems to pick the best routes. A leader for many Gogo's.
SPECIAL ABILITY:
Safe Destination
FAVOURITE GAME: Bowling

15 **BOOX**
Specializes in river crossings, but has also crossed deserts. Wow!
SPECIAL ABILITY:
Square Head
FAVOURITE GAME: Scoring

SAILEEN 16
Dreams that it is a drop of water that has evaporated and is floating among the clouds.
SPECIAL ABILITY:
Fantasy
FAVOURITE GAME: Bowling

PROFILES

HARTY 17

Its heart beats each time it discovers a new place.

SPECIAL ABILITY:
Antenna Head

FAVOURITE GAME: Scoring

18 JAHA

Gets lost a hundred times, but is always in a good mood.

SPECIAL ABILITY:
Gets Lost

FAVOURITE GAME: Bowling

19 SHEBOT

Thanks to its special suit, it can go into really hot caves.

SPECIAL ABILITY:
Heat Resistant

FAVOURITE GAME: Bowling

OFFON 20

Doesn't rest or stop, just keeps on going.

SPECIAL ABILITY:
Extra-Power

FAVOURITE GAME: Scoring

SOLFER 21

It makes up a song every time it visits a new place.

SPECIAL ABILITY:
Songwriting

FAVOURITE GAME: Bowling

22 MECHI

Very laidback and a good handyman; able to repair everything.

SPECIAL ABILITY:
Key Master

FAVOURITE GAME: K.O.

23 ENKO

If it doesn't want to be seen, it takes off its glasses and wears a mask.

SPECIAL ABILITY:
Camouflage

FAVOURITE GAME: Basket

24 MR. CAPI

If there's a new place to explore, it's the first to step forward.

SPECIAL ABILITY:
Daring Decisions

FAVOURITE GAME: Battle

PROFILES

25 AMY NICAI

Closes its eyes slowly and floats away in a dream.

SPECIAL ABILITY: Dreaming

FAVOURITE GAME: In Flight

LOSTY 26

Never remembers the way it came, and has to look for the return route.

SPECIAL ABILITY: Random Return

FAVOURITE GAME: Basket

RC-K8 27

Slides along really fast, and when it comes across an obstacle, it has to stop and use its aerial drive.

SPECIAL ABILITY: K8+ Drive

FAVOURITE GAME: In Flight

28 ZABRISKY

Has been travelling for a long time, particularly by train and knows all the routes.

SPECIAL ABILITY: Great Experience

FAVOURITE GAME: On Line

29 OIBEL

Different to all the others, it always travels by car and always arrives on time.

SPECIAL ABILITY: Punctuality

FAVOURITE GAME: Battle

SWITEL 30

Often loses the group and has to shout loudly to find them.

SPECIAL ABILITY: Shouts Loudly

FAVOURITE GAME: Battle

SCAMY 31

Spends so much time in the water, that when it comes out, it has to shout "Wait for me!"

SPECIAL ABILITY: Talks To Fish

FAVOURITE GAME: On Line

32 TAR-TAR

Tries to avoid danger so that it can keep on going and travel far.

SPECIAL ABILITY: Bravery

FAVOURITE GAME: Battle

DOC'S DATA CHECK

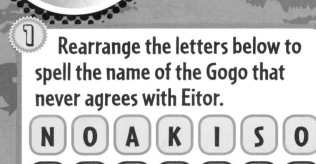

1 Rearrange the letters below to spell the name of the Gogo that never agrees with Eitor.

N O A K I S O

☐ ☐ ☐ ☐ ☐ ☐ ☐

2 Which Gogo never stops eating but always stays fit

A. Oibel ☐

B. Eitor ☐

C. Mo ☐

3

Can you name this really mixed-up Gogo?

☐

4 Although I fly, I love leaving footprints. Which Gogo am I?

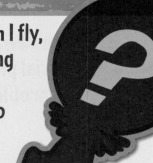

A. Doot ☐

B. Giro ☐

C. Amy Nicai ☐

5 He has a TV for a face. Can you name him?

☐

6 The Gogo's go crazy looking for him underwater, who is he?

☐

7 Who has the special ability Wonder Nose?

A. Rufus ☐

B. Raysun ☐

C. Aiko ☐

FIND ALL THE ANSWERS ON PAGE 63

FAWA'S PHOTOS!

Poor Fawa. Even though he's the Gogo's official photographer he sometimes has problems with his camera.

Can you help Fawa identify the Gogo's in the photos he's taken? It's going to take all of your drawing and colouring skills to fill in the missing details and help Fawa show off the great pictures he has taken.

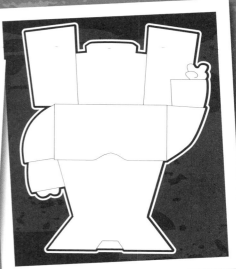

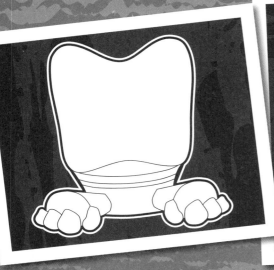

DOODLE-A-GOGO !

Time to put your drawing and colouring skills to the test. Do you know the Gogo's well enough to draw them?

Use the grids to help guide you and don't forget to use plenty of colour, you could even make up your own colour Gogo.

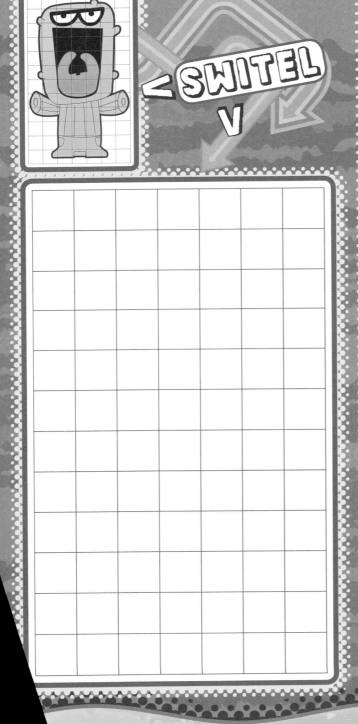

< SWITEL ∨

∧ WHAS >

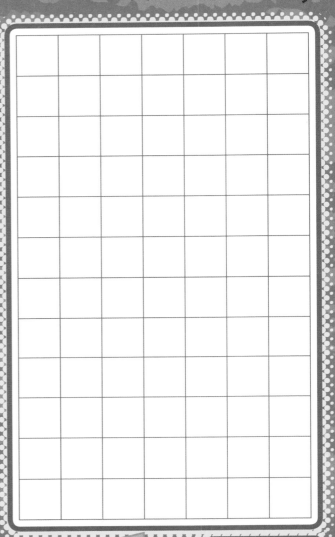

@ BONE
# TEASERS!

Satori's powers of observation are well known but even he can't spot everything. Even though he has checked them a number of times he still thinks there is something wrong with these pictures.

Can you help him out by spotting the 10 differences between these two scenes? Satori's reputation as the most watchful Gogo is on the line so make sure you find them all.

PROFILES

33 FLYCAT

Butterfly wizard. The butterflies guide it to some amazing places.

SPECIAL ABILITY:
Enchants Butterflies

FAVOURITE GAME: In Flight

FISHINO 34

Loves fish, but hates putting its feet in water... even when wearing boots!

SPECIAL ABILITY:
Cat Reflexes

FAVOURITE GAME: On Line

SARP 35

Silent and solitary. Accompanies the others, even though they can hardly see it.

SPECIAL ABILITY:
Mysterious Secret

FAVOURITE GAME: Battle

36 LASLY

Loves the small details in every place.

SPECIAL ABILITY:
Romantic Explorer

FAVOURITE GAME: K.O.

37 LUPS

Runs around everywhere. Is really fast and can sniff out even the most difficult track to follow.

SPECIAL ABILITY:
Swift Sense of Smell

FAVOURITE GAME: On Line

DUMDUM 38

Likes to be the biggest Gogo, so that it can take giant strides.

SPECIAL ABILITY:
Eats Peanuts

FAVOURITE GAME: Basket

39 GIRO

Although it flies, it loves leaving footprints everywhere it goes.

SPECIAL ABILITY:
Leaves Footprints

FAVOURITE GAME: In Flight

40 ARTIX

Travels to art museums and plays standing statues so that visitors look at it.

SPECIAL ABILITY:
Joke Artist

FAVOURITE GAME: On Line

PROFILES

UZZLE 41

Fits in everywhere and is missed when it's not around.

SPECIAL ABILITY:
Puzzle Cracker

FAVOURITE GAME: In Flight

42 GOR

Big and strong, but its slippery body can slip through small spaces.

SPECIAL ABILITY:
Strong Arm

FAVOURITE GAME: K.O.

STARFU 43

Although it's scared of exploring in the dark, it can see better at night.

SPECIAL ABILITY:
Night Explorer

FAVOURITE GAME: K.O.

44 LAMPETTI

Long-lasting and low consumption light: the ideal companion for inspecting dark places.

SPECIAL ABILITY:
Bright Light

FAVOURITE GAME: Bowling

CHENKO 45

Walks firmly and steadily, at a good pace.

SPECIAL ABILITY:
Chenko March

FAVOURITE GAME: Battle

46 EITOR

Remembers thousands of places, but finds it hard to locate them.

SPECIAL ABILITY:
Explorer Memory

FAVOURITE GAME: Scoring

47 MOKY

Likes to play jokes on others, but doesn't go too far.

SPECIAL ABILITY:
Subtle Joker

FAVOURITE GAME: Scoring

HILBO 48

Always advises his friends to have a good breakfast before setting out to explore.

SPECIAL ABILITY:
Cookie Cravings

FAVOURITE GAME: In Flight

DIN-AWA 49

Is always excited, wherever it goes.

SPECIAL ABILITY:
Happy Route

FAVOURITE GAME: Battle

50 CHATT

Doesn't stop talking the whole way. Some Gogo's complain, but nobody gets bored.

SPECIAL ABILITY:
Breaks the Silence

FAVOURITE GAME: Basket

51 CLAPPY

Wants to touch everything, and when it reaches a new place, it starts to clap.

SPECIAL ABILITY:
Quick Hands

FAVOURITE GAME: On Line

LUCKY RAB 52

Maybe it's just luck, but this Gogo never has any problems and everything always goes well.

SPECIAL ABILITY:
Very Lucky

FAVOURITE GAME: On Line

WHAS 53

Advises other Gogo's when there is any danger or when it sees something interesting to explore.

SPECIAL ABILITY:
Detects Surprises

FAVOURITE GAME: Basket

54 KICHI

Loves sweets. If it finds one, it forgets about everything else.

SPECIAL ABILITY:
Sucks Sweets

FAVOURITE GAME: Scoring

55 STARBORO

Can be seen easily from many places, and can be followed from far away.

SPECIAL ABILITY:
Guiding Star

FAVOURITE GAME: On Line

ZATOCAT 56

Has a special sense for detecting any dangers ahead.

SPECIAL ABILITY:
Detects Danger

FAVOURITE GAME: On Line

PROFILES

57 MORI
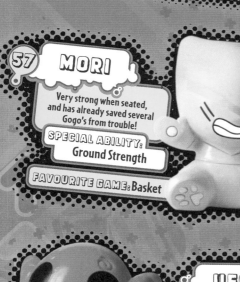
Very strong when seated, and has already saved several Gogo's from trouble!

SPECIAL ABILITY:
Ground Strength

FAVOURITE GAME: Basket

YIMO 58

Loves finding places where it can rest quietly.

SPECIAL ABILITY:
Winking Eye

FAVOURITE GAME: K.O.

UFOR 59

Nobody knows where it comes from, but it is always keen to join every adventure.

SPECIAL ABILITY:
Appears Suddenly

FAVOURITE GAME: In Flight

60 COMCO

One of Tivi's good friends. They spend the whole day playing together.

SPECIAL ABILITY:
Tests Games

FAVOURITE GAME: K.O.

61 DOC SPAVILANDER

After years of searching, it has found its favourite exploration site: the laboratory.

SPECIAL ABILITY:
Investigation

FAVOURITE GAME: Basket

TARGY 62

Likes to get to the front of the queue and give the other Gogo's something to aim for.

SPECIAL ABILITY:
Easy Target

FAVOURITE GAME: Basket

CHAMPER 63

Loves getting lost in the corners of the forest.

SPECIAL ABILITY:
Mushroom Camouflage

FAVOURITE GAME: Bowling

64 BLOCK

If Eitor sends it correct information, it can find anything straight away.

SPECIAL ABILITY:
Location Glasses

FAVOURITE GAME: Scoring

65 JOWA

Very caring.
Popular with everyone.

SPECIAL ABILITY:
Caring

FAVOURITE GAME: Basket

DIVEL 66

Bit of an urban hooligan.
Even better at skating than Tork.

SPECIAL ABILITY:
Skateboarding

FAVOURITE GAME: In Flight

DOOT 67

Always goes to the most curious
and amazing places.

SPECIAL ABILITY:
Board Games

FAVOURITE GAME: Scoring

68 NUMBAR

Has an exploration code that
hardly anyone can break.

SPECIAL ABILITY:
Key Code

FAVOURITE GAME: Basket

98326 17810 7

69 JATO

If the route is a straight line,
this Gogo is the best.

SPECIAL ABILITY:
Runs in Straight Lines

FAVOURITE GAME: Battle

70 WOLO

A little bit strange,
because although it gets seasick,
it loves travelling by boat.

SPECIAL ABILITY:
Gets Seasick

FAVOURITE GAME: K.O.

LINJAT 71

Loves climbing and finds
flat ground really boring.

SPECIAL ABILITY:
Wall Climbing

FAVOURITE GAME: K.O.

72 VLADISFOR

Has more experience than
Zabrisky and is cleverer than
Doc Spavilander, but specialises
in growing vegetables.

SPECIAL ABILITY:
Plants Lettuces

FAVOURITE GAME: On Line

PROFILES

MOBOT 73

Very well-preserved robot that also does gymnastics.

SPECIAL ABILITY: Does Not Rust

FAVOURITE GAME: Battle

74 YUCAN

Seems incredible, but many Gogo's don't know if it has three eyes or one.

SPECIAL ABILITY: Secret Eyes

FAVOURITE GAME: Battle

75 DORI MIDORI

Touches its tummy to memorize a place so that it can find it again later.

SPECIAL ABILITY: GPS Tummy

FAVOURITE GAME: Bowling

GONDO 76

By whistling and orientating its sensitive ears, it can sense if there is any water nearby.

SPECIAL ABILITY: Gentle Whistle

FAVOURITE GAME: K.O.

MIN 77

Can hypnotize a Gogo to stop it from feeling scared and to give it more energy.

SPECIAL ABILITY: Hypnotic Repair

FAVOURITE GAME: In Flight

78 GHOSTMANDER

Concentrates a lot and is very quiet. If it ever says anything, everyone listens, because it is always right.

SPECIAL ABILITY: Mental Truth

FAVOURITE GAME: In Flight

79 PLUX

Sometimes it can't decide, but shouts "forward" with its small mouth.

SPECIAL ABILITY: Indecisive

FAVOURITE GAME: Bowling

WINFLAG 80

Loves fast machines, like motorbikes, cars or motor boats.

SPECIAL ABILITY: Speed Radar

FAVOURITE GAME: Battle

GAME RULES

In flight

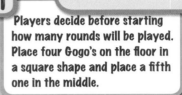

1 Players decide before starting how many rounds will be played. Place four Gogo's on the floor in a square shape and place a fifth one in the middle.

2 Take the Gogo from the middle and throw it into the air. Now try to pick up as many of the other Gogo's as you can before catching the Gogo you threw.

3 You must throw and catch the Gogo with the same hand you used to pick up the other Gogo's.

4 If the player doesn't catch the Gogo they threw up into the air, then no points are scored. Players get a point for every Gogo they pick up and the winner is the player with the most points at the end of all the rounds.

BOWLING

1 Each player must place the same number of Gogo's on the floor, about a hand width (with fingers spread) from the wall.

Bone Flip

1 Before you start, players must decide how many rounds they want to play.

2 The first player places three Gogo's in the palm of their hand, then throws them up into the air a short distance.

3 While the Gogo's are in the air, the player flips their hand over and tries to catch as many Gogo's as they can on the back of their hand. A point is scored for each Gogo successfully caught.

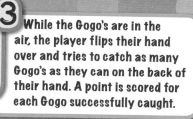

4 The next player takes their turn and this completes one round. Add another Gogo for each round that is played.

5 The winner is the player with the most points at the end of all the rounds.

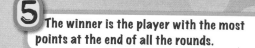

2 Take it in turns to throw a Gogo and knock over as many of your opponent's Gogo's as you can.

3 It doesn't matter if you knock down one of your own Gogo's: stand it up and carry on with the game. The player who knocks down the greatest number of their opponent's Gogo's wins the game.

gogo's CRAZY BONES — CHECKLIST

Have you got all the Gogo's? This is a list of all the Gogo's Crazy Bones® available. Use it to keep track of the ones you've got and the ones you still need to collect.

01	MOSH
02	NASAKO
03	SATO
04	OKORI
05	TORI
06	HELLY
07	SKULL
08	ANGIRU
09	UMU
10	AIKO
11	ICHIRO
12	NUCLOS
13	BOY
14	NEKO
15	HAZARD
16	SUN
17	HIRO
18	AKA

08 S

11 S

19	MOLLY
20	NARI
21	SIMI
22	CODI
23	HIRAKU
24	RUFUS
25	TEMP
26	PIBI
27	DARE
28	DANKO
29	MC TOY
30	GAIJI
31	LESSI
32	POP
33	IMON
34	JELLY
35	SUMON
36	CHO

23 S

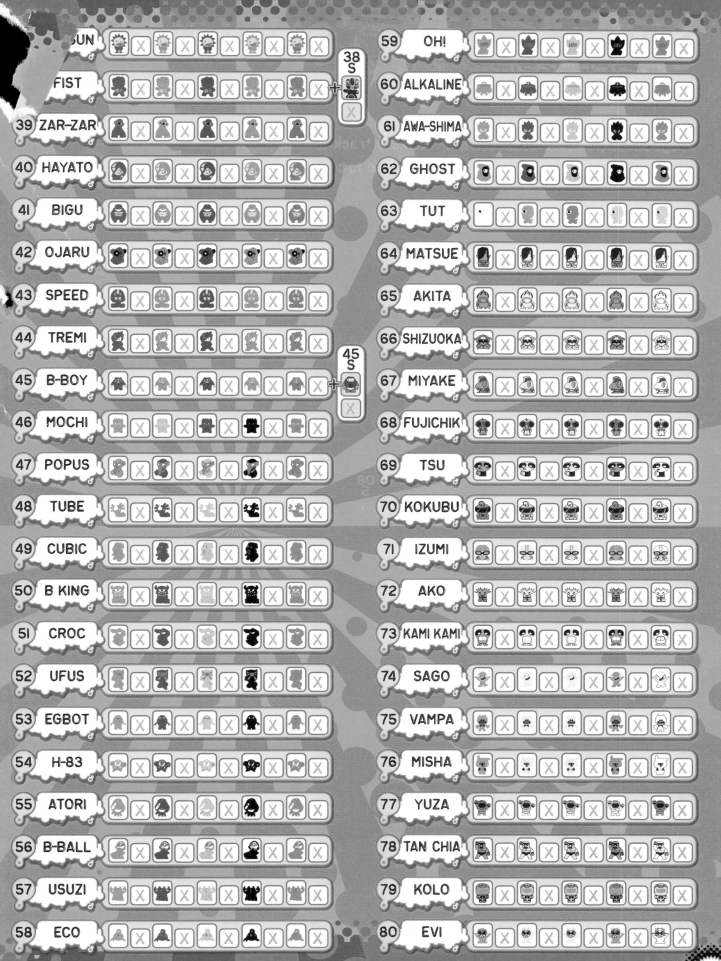

CHECKLIST

Have you got all the Gogo's? This is a list of all the Evolution Gogo's Crazy Bones® available. Use it to keep track of the ones you've got and the ones you still need to collect.

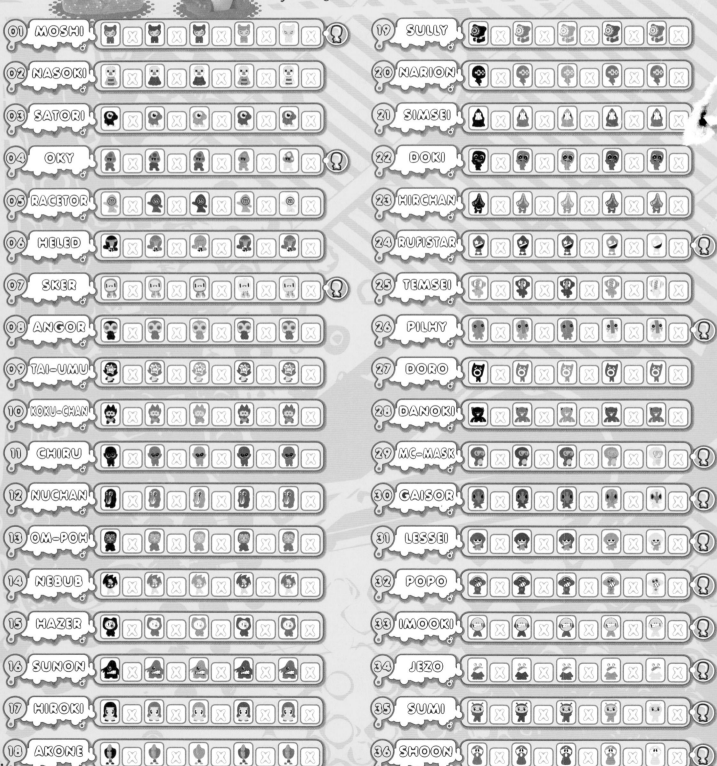

01 MOSHI
02 NASOKI
03 SATORI
04 OKY
05 RACETOR
06 HELED
07 SKER
08 ANGOR
09 TAI-UMU
10 KOKU-CHAN
11 CHIRU
12 NUCHAN
13 OM-POH
14 NEBUB
15 HAZER
16 SUNON
17 HIROKI
18 AKONE

19 SULLY
20 NARION
21 SIMSEI
22 DOKI
23 HIRCHAN
24 RUFISTAR
25 TEMSEI
26 PILHY
27 DORO
28 DANOKI
29 MC-MASK
30 GAISOR
31 LESSEI
32 POPO
33 IMOOKI
34 JEZO
35 SUMI
36 SHOON

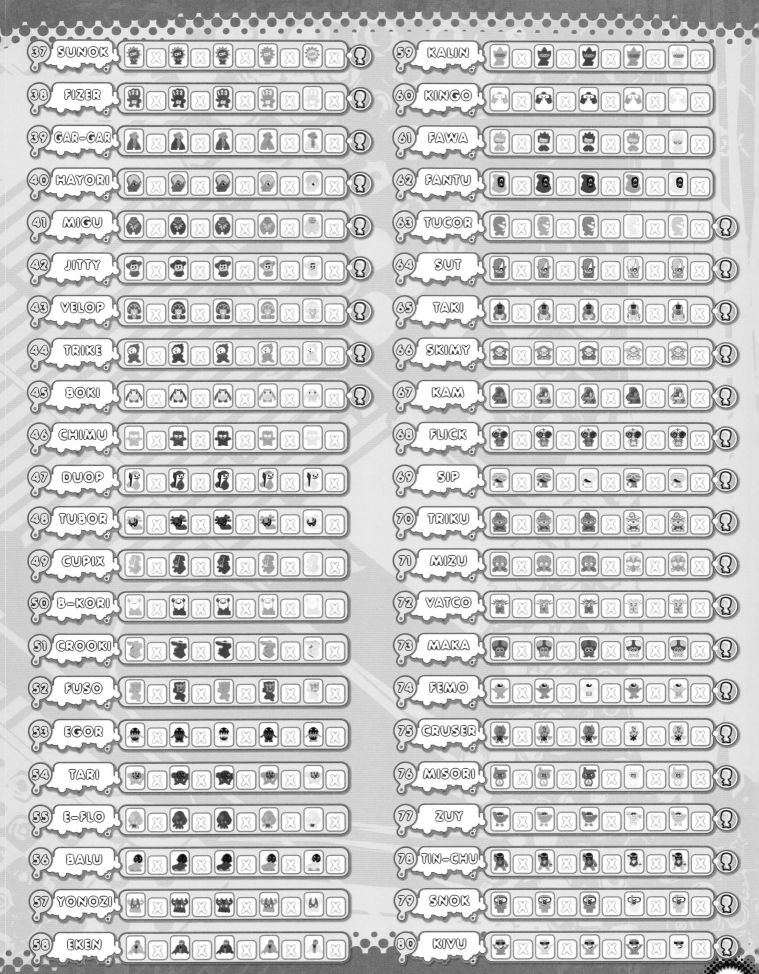

EXPLORER gogo's CRAZY BONES

CHECKLIST

Have you got all the Gogo's? This is a list of all the Explorer Gogo's Crazy Bones® available. Use it to keep track of the ones you've got and the ones you still need to collect.

01 FLAMER

02 EYDO

03 TIVI

04 XAR

05 RAYLO

06 TORK

07 BIRTU

08 MO

09 ZHIP

10 ONIKASO

11 FANBON

12 JAMPA JAMPA

13 LUNINO

14 KATO

15 BOOX

16 SAILEEN

17 HARTY

18 JAHA

19 SHEBOT

20 OFFON

21 SOLFER

22 MECHI

23 ENKO

24 MR. CAPI

25 AMY NICAI

26 LOSTY

27 RC-K8

28 ZABRISKY

29 OIBEL

30 SWITEL

31 SCAMY

32 TAR-TAR

33 FLYCAT

34 FISHINO

35 SARP

36 LASLY

58

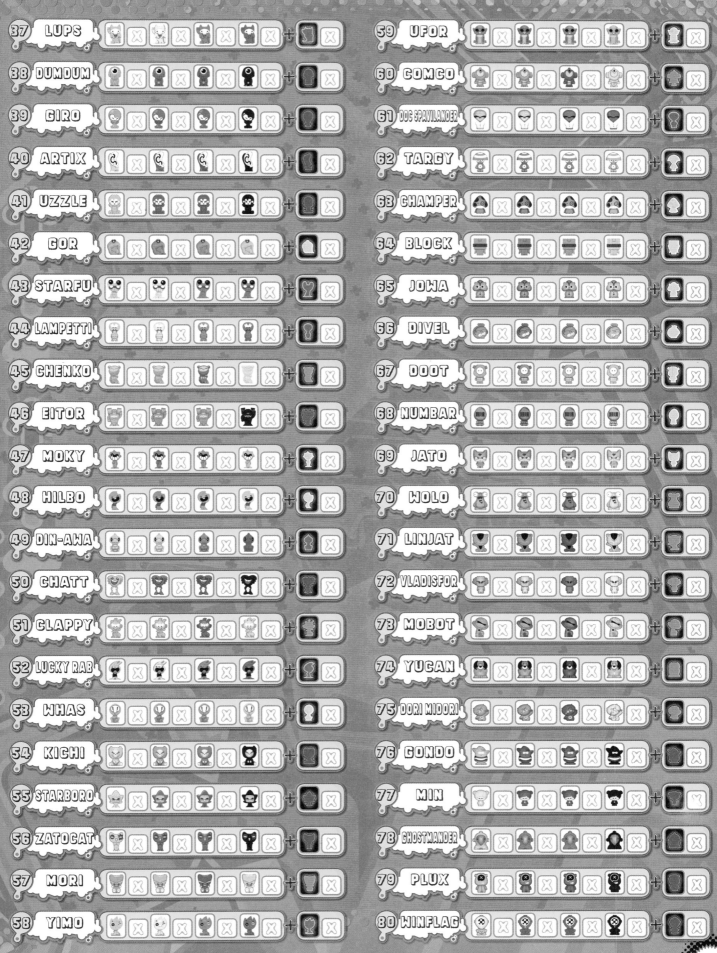

ANSWERS - ANSWERS

19 BONE TEASERS! WACKY WORDS

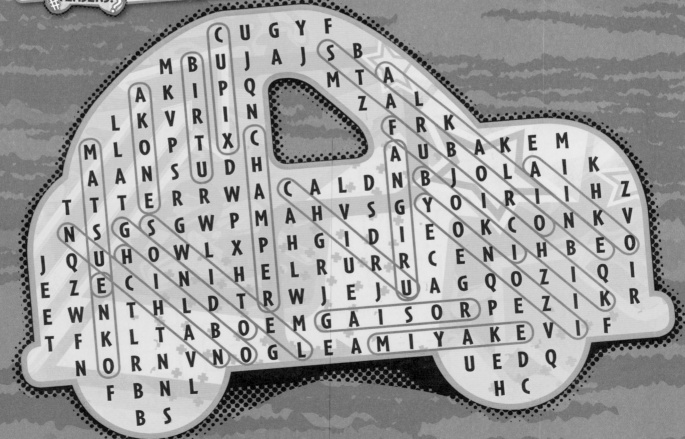

ANSWERS - ANSWERS

20 @BONE #TEASERS! GOGO° CHAOS

= 13   = 14   = 12

= 11   = 13   = 10

21 @BONE #TEASERS! LOST GOGO'S°

START

FINISH

ANSWERS - ANSWERS

27 DOC'S DATA CHECK

1. B. Cubic
2. Imooki
3. C. Lightning bolt
4. Six
5. Jowa & Fist (Special Edition)
6. Jitty
7. Nuclos - To reduce pollution

36 BONE TEASERS! WORD CROSS